MW01165708

The Church
of
Recovery

Growing in the Spiritual Life–
Dealing with Addiction and Stress

Sam Detwiler and Steve Clapp
Study Guide by Angela Zizak

Cover by Custom Maid Design

A LifeQuest Publication

The Church of Recovery

Growing in the Spiritual Life– Dealing with Addiction and Stress

Sam Detwiler and Steve Clapp
Study Guide by Angela Zizak

For further information, contact: LifeQuest, 6404 S. Calhoun Street, Fort Wayne, Indiana 46807; DadofTia@aol.com; 219-744-6510.

The authors of this book are not physicians or psychologists, and this book is not intended as a resource for persons needing medical or psychological help with addictions. This book is centered on the need of individuals for the kind of supportive community which the church at its best offers and on the need of the church to be a renewing influence for both individuals and society–out of faithfulness to Christ.

The names and/or locations of some persons in the examples in this book have been changed to protect their privacy.

Biblical quotations, unless otherwise noted, are from the New Revised Standard Version of the Bible, copyrighted 1989 by the Division of Christian Education, National Council of Churches, and are used by permission.

ISBN 1-893270-05-X

Manufactured in the United States of America

Contents

I would like to dedicate this book to my wife Floy
who supported me throughout this project. I would
also like to dedicate this book to the countless recovery
friends who showed me a better way of living and
taught me the tools I have tried to share with you.

Sam Detwiler

I dedicate this book to the congregation of Lincolnshire
Church of the Brethren, a warm and affirming people
who have transformed many lives, including mine.

Steve Clapp

We extend our thanks for the contributions made to
this book by: Kristen Leverton Helbert, Celia King,
Anne Marie Leverton, Angela Zizak, and the staff of
Evangel Press.

Ask, and it will be given you; search, and you will find; knock, and the door will be opened for you. For everyone who asks receives, and everyone who searches finds, and for everyone who knocks, the door will be opened. Is there anyone among you who, if your child asks for bread, will give a stone?

Matthew 7:7-9

Chapter One
Offering Stones to Hungry People

> *Is there anyone among you who, if your child asks for bread, will give a stone?*
>   Matthew 7:9

Some of us have the privilege of growing up in pleasant homes with affirming, loving parents. Steve Clapp describes his early years in this way:

I had a wonderful childhood. I was an only child and came along after my parents had given up on being able to have children. My mother's pregnancy was a surprise, and they were delighted by it. My middle name, Everett, was my father's first name.

My father had an entrepreneurial side and at one time owned three businesses in the small Illinois town in which I grew up: a restaurant, a tavern, and a movie theater. From a child's viewpoint, there's almost nothing as great as your family owning a movie theater! And I loved the restaurant too, especially the counter full of penny candy and the soda cooler, but all of it was fun. The movie theater, tavern, and restaurant employees liked my father and were very kind to me. When I was old enough, I got to work in the restaurant with my father and loved those experiences. In some respects, I learned more from working in the restaurant than I did from the graduate business courses I would later take. The small town tavern was not a place of heavy drinking, but my father would not let me work there and sold it while I was still in school.

My father was also politically active and was the township supervisor for many years. In those days in such a small town, that meant he was the person to whom those in financial need turned for medical help, food, and other assistance. I saw my father practice great kindness to everyone who needed help and also extend hospitality to transients who came through our town.

My mother was a high school home economics teacher and was one of the driving forces in the founding of our local library. She also had a tremendous love of animals which resulted in our giving refuge to a wide variety of orphaned or injured animals including squirrels, a raccoon, a skunk (who was de-scented one incident too late!), a screech owl, a shrew, an opossum, and a great horned owl. We always had at least one dog and at least two cats.

Both my parents were active in the church, and the Christian faith was central to their lives. They had tremendous respect for other people, and they both taught and modeled that respect to me. I also had great friends as I grew up, especially in Bruce, John, and Dick, from whom I was often almost inseparable.

There were some disadvantages to growing up in a small town, but for the most part it was a good setting. You couldn't get in very serious trouble anywhere in town without your parents finding out before you got home! With only a couple of exceptions, I had very fine teachers in elementary school, junior high, and high school.

I have made serious mistakes as an adult which brought grief to myself and those I loved. The explanations for those mistakes, however, are not to be found in my childhood. They are to be found in the depths of my own bad choices.

But not all people are so fortunate in childhood. There are those for whom a difficult childhood becomes the engine which drives them into difficult adult years. Ashley grew up in a dysfunctional home where her father sexually abused her. Her mother knew, but fearful of her husband, felt powerless to do anything about it. As she became a teenager, Ashley acted out more. She developed several addictive and compulsive behaviors that put her on the road to self-destruction. By her early twenties, she frequented bars and had casual sexual encounters with any man who would show signs of love and affection.

By the time she was 25 years old, Ashley had three significant experiences with the Christian church. The first two were negative; the third, fortunately, was positive.

Enter church experience one. Her father decided that there was something missing from his life, so he began going to church. Influenced by the church, he felt some remorse for his past behavior, but he experienced little true repentance. He did

8

not understand the depths of his daughter's pain, but he offered a half-hearted apology and insisted that she instantly respond with forgiveness. With his shallow apology, Ashley experienced many emotions–rage, hurt, and even some shame over not being able to forgive him as readily as he expected. Neither of them realized that overcoming the emotional and spiritual scars of abuse takes deep repentance, understanding, and willingness to work through both pain and shame.

About this time, Ashley was dating a boyfriend who was an abusive alcoholic. Because of the problems in their relationship, they sought help from a counselor. The counselor focused on helping the boyfriend deal with his alcoholism and on helping Ashley deal with her codependency. He recommended they both become involved in appropriate 12-step programs, which had the potential to help them make significant change. Unfortunately, their involvement with counseling and 12-step recovery was on again, off again.

Enter church experience two. Some well-meaning Christian friends entered the life of Ashley and her boyfriend. They told them they didn't need counseling or 12-step programs but simply needed to come to their church and be born again. Ashley and her boyfriend saw this as an easier, softer way; and they went for it. At first, they felt wonderful about their new-found church home and the emotional high that accompanied the born again experience. But the underlying issues were unresolved and too near the surface. Their church denied their hurt and pain–insisting their faith wasn't strong enough. The church leaders continued to lay guilt trips on them and tried to control their behavior with religious threats. They dropped out of that church.

Ashley's boyfriend had multiple affairs and one-night stands with other women and finally left Ashley. She was devastated. Overwhelmed by depression and fears, she returned to the counselor and began to deal with her codependency and the many hurts from her past. She began to experience greater self-worth, got in touch with some of her feelings, and irregularly attended church and Al-Anon (a group for family and friends of alcoholics).

Suddenly the boyfriend reappeared. He had been jilted by his latest lover and wanted Ashley back in his life. At first, she proceeded very cautiously. Then, against the advice of her counselor, she began to see him regularly. One night, in a drunken rage, he came to her apartment and insisted that she leave town with him. Forgetting her recovery work and her counselor's cautions, she went with him.

About six months later, the counselor received a desperate phone call from Ashley. Her boyfriend had left her again for another woman. She was potentially homicidal and suicidal. Desperate times required desperate measures. At their first meeting after the phone call, the counselor gave Ashley ground rules to structure her recovery:

- Attend a healthy church every Sunday.
- Attend 12-step recovery meetings regularly.
- Get a 12-step sponsor and work the steps.
- Do all the homework assignments the counselor gave her.
- Stay away from her boyfriend at all costs.

If she failed to comply with these terms, the counselor would not see her again.

Enter church experience three. She began attending the church her counselor attended and found it a loving, accepting, and healing community. When she shared some of her story with people in the church, they gave her love, not condemnation. Ashley grew in her faith and attended a Christian renewal weekend. Gaining more control over her life, she finished her undergraduate degree and went on to establish her own successful business.

(Some counselors would be reluctant to encourage a person with whom they were counseling to become involved in the same congregation. Her counselor, however, knew that church was healthy and would provide the kind of experiences which Ashley so desperately needed.)

She became cautiously involved with a man she met through a friend in church. God was central to both of their lives and in time they married and established a loving and healing Christian home. She has gone on to accept many leadership and ministry functions in the church, and her devotion to Christ is unwavering.

A Tremendous Hunger

Ashley is not atypical and represents many of the lost and broken people of our time. She had deep emotional, relational, and spiritual needs. Unfortunately, too many churches respond to people like Ashley with little understanding or even with condemnation. The intentions of the church are generally good, but people do not know how to respond. In *Sacred Chaos and the Quest for Spiritual Intimacy*, James Newby writes:

> *There is a tremendous hunger today for an experience with a God who is personal, not remote; who moves us emotionally, not merely intellectually; and whose Spirit can be a constant source of strength in a material world which is spiritually depleted. [pp. 69-70]*

Today's church often fails to meet the spiritual hunger of our time. We offer Ashley's generation, as well as those both older and younger, stones instead of bread. In other words, we often give religion ("stones") instead of spirituality ("bread"). Our religious solutions are overwhelmingly outward and fail to touch the need of the human heart and soul. As a result, we have increasing numbers of people rejecting our churches but still feeling pulled toward a deeper spiritual life.

Although many congregations are experiencing decreased attendance on Sunday morning, bookstores are filled with resources on the spiritual life, the Bible, angels, reincarnation, and related topics. The Harry Potter books by J. K. Rowling are attractive to many people in part because these stories of wizardry and magic speak to a need to transcend the materialistic experiences of daily life.

Buffy the Vampire Slayer, at the time of this writing, is an immensely popular television show for some of the same reasons. Television networks, in fact, are more willing than ever before to deal with religious themes. The series *Touched by an Angel* has enjoyed great popularity. Specials on Jesus and the life of Joan of Arc draw huge audiences.

Polls across North America show that enormous numbers of people pray daily and feel that God makes a difference in their lives. Speakers like Marianne Williamson and Thomas Moore, considered by some within the church to be "New Age," draw large crowds. Yet many people are less likely than in the past to include the institutional church as part of their spiritual seeking.

It is not our intention to criticize all of the books, speakers, resources, and movements which have appeared in secular society in response to the spiritual hunger of people. One of the authors of this book, in fact, is very fond of the Harry Potter books and feels that Thomas Moore's writings offer considerable depth and insight. It is a tragic commentary, however, that so many of our congregations have been unable to effectively address the spiritual needs of our time, especially those experienced by youth and young adults. Our churches still have enormous spiritual impact, but we are missing people we should be reaching.

No spiritual movement, outside of the church, has had an impact in society comparable to that of 12-step recovery programs. These programs have multiplied across North America without a formal organizational structure and with very few people deriving any personal financial profit from them. A few publishers and speakers who specialize in 12-step information no doubt benefit from the popularity of the 12-step movement, but the programs have a life of their own. Twelve step programs:

- Are based on sound biblical principles.

- And are highly successful in helping people overcome habits, compulsions, and dysfunctional lifestyles.

While twelve-step programs were created to help people recover, they are not to be churches or religious institutions. They use spiritual principles, but even the founders of Alcoholics Anonymous acknowledged that they were only a "spiritual kindergarten." These groups have met some needs that have been neglected by our congregations. Henri Nouwen wrote in his book *In the Name of Jesus*:

> *Many, many Christians, priests and ministers included, have discovered the deep meaning of the Incarnation not in their churches., but in the twelve steps of A.A. and A.C.A., and have come to the awareness of God's healing presence in the confessing community of those who dare to search for healing.* [p. 49]

Why do people develop addictions to alcohol and other substances? This answers to that question are complex, and a full understanding of these issues goes beyond the scope of this book. Certainly there are people like Ashley whose childhood contains at least part of the explanation. There are others, however, who not only have a good childhood but also a good adult life yet still struggle with addiction.

Peer pressure certainly is part of the problem for those whose acquaintance or friendship circles in school or in work include people who regularly abuse alcohol or other drugs. There is some evidence that certain people are more subject to addictions than others, as though there is in part a genetic or biological basis for a predisposition to such problems. Some persons become addicted to alcohol during a time of deep personal grief, and there are people who become addicted to prescription pain-killers during recovery from serious injury.

The truth is that there are multiple causes for conditions such as alcoholism. Whatever the root of the cause for any individual person, there remains substantial evidence that 12-step programs can provide the framework for recovery for enormous numbers of people. All of us can benefit from that framework. While it may be true that some of us have been spared major addictions, it is also true that we all deal with some degree of brokenness. We all need healing, and that reality will be discussed more thoroughly as this book continues.

Spirituality and Religion

Spirituality is not the same as religion. **Spirituality is having a healthy, dynamic, and growing relationship with God, self, and others.** Growing intimacy in all of these relationships feeds the hunger, loneliness, and alienation of the human soul. This intimacy is at the heart of the Christian message. This definition of spirituality is implicit in the teachings of Jesus. When asked what the greatest commandment was, Jesus responded:

> *You shall love the Lord your God with all your heart,*
> *and with all your soul, and with all your mind. This*
> *is the greatest and the first commandment. And a*
> *second is like it: You shall love your neighbor as*

13

> yourself. *On these two commandments hang all the law and the prophets."* Matthew 22:37b-40

Our lives need to be centered first on love of God, and all our love of others flows out of our relationship with God. This passage is not about a self-centered, desire-filled, emotionally-based love for others. Jesus is talking about loving others in the same way as God loves us. He is speaking of loving without a desire to control and of continuing to love even in the face of adversity and offensive behavior. He is speaking of love which seeks the highest possible good for the other person. This love is action born of decision, not an impulse born out of emotions. It is a healthy, dynamic, and growing love.

Our love needs to flow to God, to others, and to ourselves. Jesus clearly tells us that our love for God must be more than emotional and transitory but must involve the deepest resources of the heart, soul, and mind. A reflection of such love is found in how we love others–our neighbors. Jesus calls us to love our neighbors–not instead of or more than–but in the same way as we love ourselves.

The lost, the broken, the dysfunctional, and the addicted all have one thing in common: self-hatred. Successful recovery includes learning to love one's self in a constructive and spiritual manner. Experienced participants in twelve-step programs often say that they are there to love newcomers until those persons learn to love themselves.

In reality, we cannot love others, knowing their hurts and needs, unless we have first learned to love ourselves. A healthy love of ourselves, with all of our shortcomings and failures, is absolutely necessary if we are to have a healthy love of others, with all of their shortcomings and failures. There is a strong interdependency between our love of ourselves and our love of others. Spirituality is having a healthy, dynamic, and growing relationship with God, self, and others.

If this is spirituality, what then is religion? **Religion is the system of rites, beliefs, and behaviors that enables spirituality to thrive and grow in the person and in the faith community.** Religion can be healthy or unhealthy. At an ideal level, religion fosters spirituality. But too often, religion is either irrelevant to spirituality or damages it, as seen in Ashley's story. *Religion must be the servant of spirituality, and not the other way around.* Here are some ways in which religion can be unhealthy.

First, religion can shelter us from the realities of life. We have all heard of persons who are so heavenly minded that they are no earthly good. Too often churches are used as hide-outs and not sanctuaries. People come not to deal with the problems which are part of daily living, but to run away from them. Christians become so involved in church activities, that they forget to live out the gift of humanity that God has given them. In a workshop Sam attended on "Spirituality and Leadership," Roy Oswald, senior consultant for the Alban Institute, stated: "Spirituality is how you perceive reality."

Many churches enthusiastically embark on ministries to the lost and broken without thinking about what it would mean to truly welcome those people into the life of the church. It is sometimes easier to think about ministries *to* broken people than *with* broken people. Church members whose own lives have been comparatively sheltered may be uncertain how to relate to those who have experienced alcoholism, drug addiction, imprisonment, bankruptcy, and other major problems. They don't mean to be unfriendly, but they falsely believe that they do not know how to relate to those who have been so broken. With this myth in mind, they never pursue deeper friendship with broken newcomers. They never discover that broken people have a lot to offer them, and they may also be blinded to the areas of brokenness which exist even in the lives of the most fortunate people. Churches can become divided communities with traditional church members in one group and "recovery" people in the other group. These churches are not "one body in Christ" and are prime candidates for division and conflict.

Second, religion can be overly rational and not experiential. As Christianity moved from the mystical East to the rational West, rationality became something of an idol for many in the church. Faith seems to focus on what can be rationally understood and explained, while mystical and supernatural experiences are discarded as unsophisticated and simplistic. We can fall into the trap of trying to localize our concept of God in a box of rationality, forgetting that God cannot be confined to an ideology of our manufacture or imagination. In *The Emerging American Church*, Dan Scott, pastor of Valley Cathedral in Phoenix, Arizona has written:

> *A new generation of American nonbelievers are. . .*
> *incurably spiritual. They have rejected the rationalism*
> *of their parents all their lives. Their deepest*
> *concerns have become more closely connected with*
> *our Christian faith than previous generations. And*
> *yet they are turning inward and to the Far East for*
> *solace, because they simply cannot connect with a*
> *Christian rationalism that offers answers to questions*
> *they are not asking. American Christianity must come*
> *to grips with this fundamental cultural change.* [p. 211]

Third, we can become trapped into thinking that outwardly religious behavior reflects an inner spiritual depth. Religion, of course, *should be* an outward representation of an inward spiritual reality; unfortunately, we too often emphasize the former and neglect the latter. Jesus warned his disciples about the Pharisees who showed a lot of outwardly religious behavior but had little real spirituality behind it. Jesus taught that our righteousness must exceed that of the Pharisees [Matthew 5:20, et.al.].

Religious behavior cannot make us spiritual. We can no more become Christians by spending time in church than we can become automobiles by sleeping in a garage. Spirituality requires a transformation that is born within a person's life. Religious behavior, at its best, can be a catalyst and a support system for these spiritual and transformational experiences–and religious behavior can also reflect the results of those experiences.

Fourth, religion often fails to meet the deepest needs of the human soul. In his challenging book *The Secret Life of the Soul*, Keith Miller suggests that each of us has constructed an outer personality which has been unconsciously designed to meet the needs and demands of the shaming and demanding voices all around us. Meanwhile, we each have an inner child or an inner soul whose needs and hungers are often overlooked and ignored in order to conform to the expectations of others. The imprisoned soul within each of us cries out desperately–leaving us feeling restless, empty, and dissatisfied with life. Keith Miller offers this insight: "It is our soul that guides us to become real, and that yearns for God and his reality and way of persistent integrity" [p. 25].

We are created in the image of God, and the soul reflects the complexity and wonder of the Creator. In some respects, the spiritual life is a pilgrimage toward a deeper understanding of the soul and its relationship to God. Sam shares these discoveries which he has made about his own soul:

- My soul is the part of me that feels innocent and childlike before God as my heavenly Father–*Abba*. That reality takes nothing away from the importance of feminine images of God.

- My soul is the part of me that generates a creative force which impels me to grow, develop, and make new things.

- My soul is the part of me that finds wonder in a Rocky Mountain vista or a beautiful sunset in the Midwest.

- My soul is the part of me that desires true intimacy with God, myself, and others.

- My soul is the part of me that shuns complexity and seeks the depths of simplicity.

- My soul is the part of me that wants to enjoy life and laugh with a Godly humor.

- My soul is the part of me that desires a life with meaning and purpose and seeks to respond to God's call.

- My soul is the part of me that feels burdened and oppressed by sin and shame and that craves divine grace to cleanse and heal me.

- My soul is the part of me that recognizes my true worth is not in my accomplishments, but in my relationship with God.

You may wish to spend time reflecting on how you would describe your own soul. That process is literally the work of a lifetime. Our true spiritual needs are defined by the soul, not by religious institutions.

There is a Christian persona that can be shaped by the conforming and shaming voices of the Christian community. While people are sincere when they accept the Christian faith, it's deceptively easy to end up playing Christian roles instead of becoming all that God has created each person to be. The busy-ness of the congregation and the expectations of church members can easily take us on a religious journey rather than a spiritual journey.

Fifth, religion can be superficial and keep us from seeing the big picture for the church or for our own lives. It's easy in the church to ask "How can we ever do that?" instead of asking "What is God's vision for us?" Christians sometimes get hung up on what clothes are worn to church rather than recognizing our need to be clothed with Christ. Instead of dis-cussing the color of God's love in our hearts and lives, we talk about the color of the carpet in the fellowship hall. Many people in established congregations grow weary of the seemingly endless meetings required to make relatively small decisions when they are wanting to be involved in feeding the hungry, working with youth, or sharing the faith.

There have obviously been many approaches to the renewal of the church and of individual spiritual lives. Some of those have been effective in some churches, but we continue to live in a time of great spiritual hunger. In order to adequately deal with that hunger, the church needs to be transformed in how it practices religion.

In this book we invite you to explore with us what the church can learn from 12-step programs. It is not our contention that the 12-step movement is without fault or that it is superior to what thousands of congregations in North America offer each week. We both know and have shared in the life of congregations which do a wonderful job nourishing the soul and reaching out in the name of Christ. Although the ideals of the 12-step programs are both noble and biblical, there are a few 12-step groups which have become unhealthy. Overall, however, the 12-step movement has been successful in North America in large part because of its strong impact on the spiritual lives of participants. There are things we can learn from these groups which can help in the renewal of congregational life and help us better understand how to reach out to others. While 12-step groups minister to particular kinds of brokenness, the reality is that all of us are broken in a variety of ways–some ways are simply more apparent than others.

This book is not about the incorporation of 12-step groups into the life of the church but about finding new ways for the church to effectively nourish the spiritual life and reach out with Christ's love. It is time the church gave bread, not stones, to those who are spiritually hungry. And we are all spiritually hungry.

The box which follows lists the twelve steps of A.A. The steps as originally written used the male pronoun alone to refer to God. Because many using this book are more comfortable with female than male images of God, we have slightly modified the steps to avoid use of male or female pronouns, knowing in our hearts that God is beyond all our efforts at description but that words remain valuable tools.

**The Twelve Steps
Adapted from Alcoholics Anonymous**

1. We admitted we were powerless over our hurts, hang-ups, and habits–that our lives had become unmanageable.
2. Came to believe that a Power greater than ourselves could restore us to sanity.
3. Made a decision to turn our will and our lives over to the care of God.
4. Made a searching and fearless moral inventory of ourselves.
5. Admitted to God, to ourselves, and to another human being, the exact nature of our wrongs.
6. Were entirely ready to have God remove all these defects of character.
7. Humbly asked God to remove our shortcomings.
8. Made a list of all persons we had harmed, and became willing to make amends to them all.
9. Made direct amends to such people wherever possible, except when to do so would injure them or others.
10. Continued to take personal inventory and when we were wrong promptly admitted it.
11. Sought through prayer and meditation to improve our conscious contact with God, praying only for knowledge of God's will for us and the power to carry that out.
12. Having had a spiritual awakening as the result of these steps, we tried to carry the message to other broken people, and to practice these principles in all our affairs.

Chapter Two
The Need for Healing

> But when (Jesus) heard this, he said, "Those who are
> well have no need for a physician, but those who are
> sick."   Matthew 9:12

Sam Detwiler shares this story about his friend Charlie, a man known for years as a drunk: *Charlie had been arrested many times on charges related to his drinking problem, but one arrest brought a different consequence. As part of his sentence, he was required to go to Alcoholics Anonymous. Charlie found, to his surprise, that he liked going to the meetings because he enjoyed the people and found solace in being sober.*

In light of his past, this seemed almost unbelievable. Charlie had lived in a dozen different states. He was essentially homeless and without family support for years. In one state, he found a woman he really loved named Annie; and he moved in with her. They were together as common law mates over 20 years. She moved with him many times but finally insisted they settle down.

They lived in a trailer in a small farming town of 2,000 people and eventually had two children. Because of his drinking episodes, Charlie wasn't much of a father, husband, or family man. He worked off and on at odd jobs, barely making enough for his family to survive, with most of the money going for alcohol. But then the miracle happened. Through the spiritual program of Alcoholics Anonymous, Charlie got sober. By this time his Annie was terminally ill with cancer, and his son had also become an alcoholic. Life was further complicated by the reality that Charlie's own health was not good. His kidneys were practically gone, requiring dialysis three times a week. His heart was barely functional. But he was alive, and he was sober. He even brought his alcoholic son with him to meetings on occasion.

At AA, people loved Charlie. He was always friendly and greeted everyone in the room. He would talk your ear off, but he was so good natured, nobody seemed to mind. If newcomers came, Charlie was the first to offer words of encouragement and to help them. He would often say to them, "Now I want you to keep coming back, and stay away from the booze. It'll kill you."

When Annie died from her cancer, Charlie was devastated. His friends at AA supported him in his grief, and he used the spiritual principles to help him stay sober. He helped his son get into detox and drove him to as many meetings as he could. Charlie's own health continued to deteriorate–too many years of hard drinking had destroyed his body beyond repair.

Charlie visited with me about his spiritual concerns because he knew I was a pastor who was supportive of AA groups. He said, "Sam, my health isn't so good. I know my days are numbered. And I want to be with Annie again when I leave this world. I miss her a lot." He wanted to grow closer to Christ, and he wanted to be sure he was ready for heaven. I reassured him that he had come to the right place to get sober by coming to AA but that a church could help him in his desire to be certain of his salvation. I invited him to my church and was amazed when he said "Yes."

The next Sunday, Charlie walked into church. He came dressed as usual–a dirty flannel shirt, torn jeans, old beat-up cowboy boots, and an unshaven face. But I didn't care. He was where he needed to be. The people of the church disregarded his unkempt appearance and welcomed him warmly. The elderly women of the church especially enjoyed fussing over him. He told me later how much that meant to him. Recovery people in the church who knew him from meetings did everything they could to make him feel welcome.

Charlie came to church about every other week, always dressed in the same way. One woman asked me, "How did you get Charlie to come to church?" My reply was simple: "I invited him." Charlie discovered that our church had lots of potluck dinners, so he often stayed afterwards to enjoy the food and the companionship. He always took a big plateful of food. He said, "I know I'll pay for this in my kidney dialysis tomorrow, but I don't care. This food is too good to pass up."

Then Charlie had his first heart attack. When I visited him in the hospital, we began to talk about deeper spiritual issues. But Charlie was too busy talking to listen very well. He was upset because he was in the hospital and would miss his grand-daughter's birthday party. He arranged to send her a birthday *cake. When hospital staff determined that there was little they could do for Charlie, they dismissed him.*

A month later, Charlie suffered a more severe heart attack. When I visited him, Charlie was not his talkative self. The physicians were talking about doing a heart catheterization, but he wasn't sure he wanted to go through it. He finally said in exasperation, "Sam, my old heart is worn out." We sat together quietly for a time thinking about Charlie's situation.

Breaking the silence, I said, "Charlie, I don't know very much about medicine, but I think the best thing for your heart right now is to make sure Jesus is in it." I knew he had grown spiritually through AA and that his church experiences had helped him as well, but I wasn't certain he had fully committed himself to Christ. He smiled at me and replied, "Sam, because you have been such a good friend to me, I believe you. I'll take care of that right away." We prayed together, and I left. That evening a recovering alcoholic from our church visited Charlie. She noticed a great difference in him. He had a peace about him she had never seen before. She left and within a half hour, another friend from AA came to see him. While he was there, Charlie died.

The funeral service for Charlie was unlike any I had experienced. There were church people with no apparent addictions sitting alongside those who had found sobriety in AA along with Charlie. There were also people there who would still be described by many as drunks and who had not been in a church for years. I used the biblical story of the repentant thief on the cross to talk about Charlie. I talked about the things he had done wrong and about the suffering he had experienced before getting sober. Then I talked about all the things he had done right since he had become sober and about the many people he had helped and encouraged. Finally, I talked about his acceptance of Jesus Christ and his relationship with God.

Charlie got to see Annie again, not because he knew sobriety, but because he knew God. I feel confident he is sitting at the feast of the kingdom drinking all the heavenly wine he wants. His disease of alcoholism is completely healed, along with all the other brokenness in his life.

Tears come to my eyes as I write about my friend Charlie. We all get goose bumps when we hear about people like Charlie doing a complete turnaround with God's help and the encouragement of others. We don't always recognize the relevance of their stories to the stories of our own lives. We gratefully acknowledge the wonderful things that happened to Charlie, but we never think it will happen for us. Many of us don't think we need transformation and renewal as badly as someone like Charlie does.

We Are All Broken People

The reality is that we are all broken people. We are just broken in different ways. John Baker, Pastor of Celebrate Recovery at Saddleback Church in Lake Forest, California, believes that not only is everyone in society broken, but also everyone in the church. He sees too many people, including Christians, trying to fill the emptiness within them using other things in place of Christ. People outside the church may be more likely to use alcohol, drugs, sex, and gambling to fill that emptiness. Those same problems exist in the lives of people who are active in the church; but many in the church may be more likely to use self-will power, self-righteousness, workaholism, and compulsive overeating. All of these things are evidence of brokenness that comes from sin.

When Sam worked as an alcohol and drug counselor, he was invited to speak with a college psychology class about addiction. He began by asking the class how many were addicted to something. Not a hand was raised. Then he began to bring the issue closer to their lives:

- How many smoked a pack of cigarettes a day?
  Some hands went up.

- How many ate compulsively?
  More hands went up.

- How many were compulsive doers or workaholics?
  More hands went up.

He continued to list addictive behaviors and compulsions, and hands kept going up. He kept a tally on the chalkboard; and by the end of the inventory, there were three times as many addictions and compulsions as there were people in the room. Addiction and brokenness are far more prevalent than we think.

Newsweek reported in the year 2000 the estimate, based on U.S. Government statistics, that six million American children are overweight enough to endanger their health [June 25, 2000]. In 2001, the U.S. Department of Health and Human Services estimated that over five million girls and women and over one million boys and men suffer from eating disorders.

People in many fields in North America are working more and more hours and displaying more signs of being addicted to their work. Between 1977 and 1997, the average workweek went from 43 hours to 47 hours, according to statistics in *U.S. News and World Report* [December 20, 1999]. During that same period, the percentage working 50 or more hours a week climbed from 25 percent to 37 percent. According to the General Social Survey in Canada, fully one-third of Canadians between the ages of 25 and 44 self-identified as workaholics; and over half expressed concern about not having enough time with friends and family.

With men and women both working in most two-parent families, it is not unusual for both parents to arrive home after 7 p.m. in the evening and feel overwhelmed by the household and parenting tasks before them. Exhaustion and irritability are the order of the day for some families. Single parents, with the total responsibility for producing income and managing the household, can feel an even greater sense of pressure. This isn't to say that all people who work long hours are addicted to their work, and it certainly isn't intended as a criticism of single parents who can't escape heavy economic pressures. It is, however, easy to become addicted to work and to the production of as much income as possible.

Alcoholism, which motivated the initial formation of 12-step groups, continues to have tragic impact in North America. In the United States, that is most strikingly reflected in traffic fatalities. In 1999, of 41,611 U.S. traffic deaths, almost 38% were alcohol-related. The chart which follows shows the trend on overall traffic fatalities and on those which are alcohol-related in the United States. There is evidence that both the U.S. and Canada are making progress in reducing alcohol-related fatalities, through education, law enforcement, and safety devices such as air bags; but the loss of life is still staggering. Between 1982 and 1999, the percentage of traffic fatalities in the United States which were alcohol-related decreased from 57.3% to 37.9%; but there were still 15,786 deaths which could have been avoided if people did not drink and drive. And these statistics represent only one measure of problems from alcohol. Lost work production, shattered families, depression, and suicide can often be directly attributed to alcohol problems.

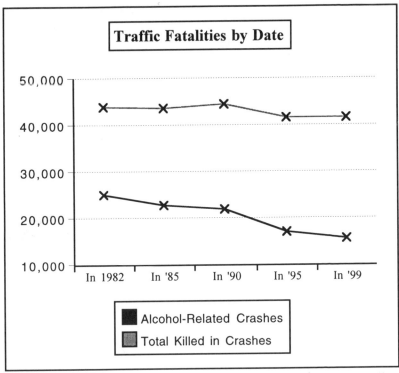

The above data comes from the U.S. Department of Transportation

Then there are addictions to power, to judgmentalism, to anger, and to the accumulation of wealth, which are harder to measure statistically but which clearly impact large numbers of people in North America. Addiction and brokenness have impact on all of our lives.

Our Need for Healing

The Greek word for salvation in the Bible literally means "healing." We need to be healed physically, emotionally, relationally, and spiritually. We need more than an absence of pain. We need a spirit of wholeness and completeness. In the church, we have become accustomed to thinking about Jesus saving us from our sin. Many of us, like Sam's friend Charlie, want to be right with God so that we are prepared for heaven. But salvation, properly understood, is a far broader concept and concerns this life as well as the life to come. Jesus saves us from our sins; but Jesus also heals us from our brokenness.

Many Christians today talk about "saving souls." While their intentions are good, they fail to realize that the idea of separating the body from the mind and soul is a Western idea, not a biblical one. In the Old Testament, the Jewish people never divided us into different parts. We were considered to be one. Therefore, Old Testament ideas of God's salvation could include anything from deliverance from bondage in Egypt to David being forgiven his sins with Bathsheeba. When we look at ourselves holistically instead of in separate parts, we realize that God's salvation is for our souls, our bodies, our relationships, and many other aspects of our lives.

Alan Richardson, in *The Interpreter's Dictionary of the Bible*, reminds us that God acts in history through ordinary people in order to bring the message of salvation: "Salvation history is the story of the divine action for our salvation in and through the lives and persons of real flesh-and-blood historical characters, as sensual and as fallible as [people] usually are, and yet who were, through no virtue of their own, made the instruments of the divine plan for the salvation of the world" [Vol. 4, p. 171]. God acts in this life to heal us and to rescue us from destruction, and God assures us of greater salvation which is to come.

You might want to put the book aside for a few moments and think about the things from which God has already saved you and about the areas in which you would still like to experience that salvation. Sam offers this list from his own life:

- Jesus saved me from addictive and compulsive behavior that was destroying me.
- Jesus saved me from never feeling that I am good enough.
- Jesus saved me from loneliness and helped me have healthier relationships.

- Jesus saved me from excessive self-centeredness that left me empty.
- Jesus saved me from self-punishing, unrelenting shame.
- Jesus saved me from impulsive behavior patterns.
- Jesus saved me from going too fast and pushing too hard.

Of course salvation in many areas is not a single, one-time event but rather a process that continues through one's life. And salvation is about more than healing our brokenness–it is about enabling us to more effectively reach out with Christ's love to others. We need healing not only for ourselves but for our ministry to others.

The oversimplification of salvation causes some to espouse a one-step recovery process. They say: "Just go to the altar, confess your sins, ask Jesus into your heart, and everything will be fine." Those persons see 12-step recovery programs as over-complicating the salvation process. They don't understand why alcoholics need to keep going to AA and why compulsive over-eaters need to keep going to Overeaters Anonymous. Salvation is a process, and staying healed of some afflictions and addictions requires a continuing commitment and the support of others. We are saved, but saved for a purpose. Healing our brokenness and fulfilling our purpose are lifelong challenges and opportunities.

Many of us, of course, have avoided facing our own brokenness. We need to be reminded of the words of Christ: "Those who are well have no need for a physician, but those who are sick" [Matthew 9:12]. Our failure to recognize our own need of the Great Physician has harmed us individually and the church as the body of Christ in at least three ways:

First, we cannot be healed if we do not know we are sick. It may be alcoholism or another drug addiction. It may be a destructive temper. It may be difficulty maintaining healthy relationships. It may be unbridled shame. It may be an addiction to work or to the accumulation of wealth. It may be a fixation on power and control. It may be excessive judgmentalism or jealousy. It may be a sexual addiction or compulsion. But until we recognize and acknowledge our brokenness, we are not able to claim the healing Christ offers.

Second, not acknowledging our own brokenness may damage those who worship alongside us. When we are able to speak frankly about our brokenness, we make it easier for others to do the same. Fearful of seeming like inferior Christians, people hide their brokenness, hoping no one will discover it. When one person acknowledges the need for healing, it becomes easier for others to do the same.

Those who work with small groups in the church know what a difference is made in group life when one member opens his or her heart and shares a significant need or problem. The others in the group are quick to be supportive of the one who has shared, but much more begins to happen. Group members, who were initially reluctant to share their deepest hurts and needs, find themselves able to do so because of the courage and faith of the first person who was open.

Third, our witness suffers when we hide our brokenness. We truly live in a broken world filled with broken people. Those outside the church won't come in if they see themselves as inferior to those in the congregation or if they suspect that there is a spirit of judgmentalism rather than of acceptance in the church. How can we tell about Jesus who completely heals and saves us unless we have fully experienced it in all areas of our own lives?

Elaine was one of the most successful pastors in her denomination. She began her ministry in a congregation of only 53 persons, but there was ample opportunity to reach newcomers since the church was located near a new housing development. Elaine's enthusiasm and commitment to outreach energized the entire congregation; and in a five year period of time, the church grew to 186 members. She provided the leadership for significant growth in the next congregation she pastored, and then she found herself the senior pastor of a church with 1,750 members. That church, however, had once been much larger, almost 4,000 members, and had been in steady decline for 25 years.

Elaine found herself working more hours and growing more frustrated that she could not reverse the decline of the church. People in the congregation had high expectations because of her past success, and she began to feel like a failure. She became more irritable with her husband and children, and she began making impossible demands on the rest of the staff. Elaine felt that she was letting everyone down, including God.

Always an avid runner and pleased with her health, Elaine was taken by surprise when she felt nauseous and then collapsed while running on a track in a health club. She was taken to the emergency room where she was diagnosed with high blood pressure and put on medication. She took the next four days off, prayed, and reassessed her life. The following Sunday, instead of a prepared sermon, Elaine talked openly and frankly to the congregation about her sense of failure over not being able to reverse the decline in the church. She acknowledged that she had become an unpleasant person to her family and the church staff, and she said that she did not know if it was possible to reverse the decline. She did know that her health and her outlook were suffering and that she had to slow her pace, rely more on other people, and turn her own life over more fully to God.

Elaine's candor and openness had a tremendously healing impact on the congregation. Several members began to talk to her and to each other about their own workaholic personalities and unfair expectations. She began to see healing in her own life, and her openness helped others to recognize their need for healing.

Salvation and recovery are not one-time events but a process and a lifestyle. Noel Gerlich, a member of the pastoral care staff at Valley Cathedral in Phoenix, Arizona, says that "God has a restoration program for each and every one of us." She explains that it is always God who gives salvation, but there are times when that salvation comes to people through the 12-step recovery process.

All our brokenness is not immediately healed, and our purpose in life tends to come to us in small steps rather than in a single revelation. God walks with us through the days of our lives; and God works through others to strengthen, heal, and guide us. Some of the most significant healing for many people has come through 12-step recovery groups, but that healing also comes in other settings and sometimes through unlikely people. We are called to share God's good news of salvation and healing with one another–in 12-step groups, in the overall life of the church, and in our daily lives.

Chapter Three
The Need for Grace

> ... all have sinned and fall short of the glory
> of God.   Romans 3:23

Gabe had been raised in a strict, Bible-based church. His father was a lay speaker, a respected church leader, and a very demanding, controlling person. When Gabe was 18 years old, he rebelled against the religiosity and rigid expectations which had been forced on him. Like the prodigal son wanting to go his own way, he joined the Merchant Marines and went off to see the world.

In his journeys, he engaged in pleasures his strict parents had prohibited. He developed a deep resentment for the church and all of the hypocrisy found in it, which seemed to him justification for his behavior. In every port, he found a different sin to indulge. He finally felt free from all the inhibitions and rules that had been imposed upon him, and he enjoyed these prohibited pleasures for decades. But like the prodigal son, Gabe found that the pleasures carried a high price.

Some thirty years later, Gabe returned to his hometown. He had severe diabetes and the body of a 75-year-old, though he was still in his fifties. His many years of wild living had taken a heavy toll on him. His parents were dead, and he lived in a small house by himself. He found work in the parts department of an automobile dealership.

Because of his poor health, Gabe was a frequent patient in the local hospital. Most nurses hated taking care of him because of his bitter and demanding disposition. Sam often visited Gabe in the hospital. Gabe was always glad to see him, and their visits were generally pleasant. But whenever Sam mentioned the Christian faith, Gabe went off on an angry tirade about everything he thought was wrong with the church.

A crisis came when Gabe accidentally spilled boiling water on his foot while preparing his dinner at home. Because of his diabetes, it would not heal, and he had to be hospitalized. The foot proved very difficult to treat, and there was talk of possible amputation. At this point, Gabe was pessimistic about his future. During one of their visits, Sam offered to anoint Gabe for healing (James 5:14-16). Sam suggested that Gabe's guilt and shame over his past actions could be blocking his healing. At first, Gabe was cynical and scoffed at those "crazy faith healers on television."

Sam visited Gabe again the next day, which was Good Friday. As Sam started to leave, Gabe meekly asked, "Would you anoint me for healing?" Sam quickly found some oil and enlisted the help of a church leader who was visiting a woman down the hall from Gabe's room.

They began the service by asking Gabe to share any sins he felt a need to confess. The church leader blushed as they heard a list of sins not often acknowledged in the presence of others. Gabe was open and honest about his past. They then anointed him, laid hands on him, and prayed for him. As they prepared to leave, Sam said, "Gabe, all your sins are forgiven." In awe, he responded, "That almost seems too good to be true."

Gabe began experiencing grace and healing immediately. First, his attitude was healed. The nurses in the hospital began to ask each other, "What's wrong with Gabe? He's acting so nice." Then there was evidence that Gabe's broken relationship with God was healing. He requested a pass from his doctor to go to church that Easter Sunday. Sam's wife, who was a physician at the hospital, was glad to give him a ride to church. For the first time in many years, Gabe truly worshipped God within the Christian community.

Gabe's physical healing also came quickly. Within two days, the burn on his foot was down to the size of a quarter; and in less than a week, it was completely gone. His agnostic doctor speculated that "the medicine I was giving him must have finally worked." But the rest of us suspected another explanation. And finally, Gabe's broken relationship with the church was healed. After his release from the hospital, Gabe was in church every Sunday where he became involved in activities and later became treasurer. Church was home to him again.

Gabe died and now lives fully in God's care; but his story remains a vivid illustration of repentance, forgiveness, and grace. The heart of the Gospel is not ethics, or church activities, or even Bible study. Those are all important aspects of our faith, but the true heart of the Gospel is grace. Grace is a gift of acceptance and new life which comes to us out of the immense love of God rather than because we deserve to receive it. *But God proves his love for us in that while we were still sinners Christ died for us* (Romans 5:8).

The Reality of Sin

Many in 12-step programs fear that the sins in their past will affect how people will treat them at church, and that often makes them reluctant to become involved. It's easy for those of us in the church to fall into the trap of judgmentalism and to fail to see the desperate need of those seeking recovery. But a focus on grace radically transforms our approach to God and our view of others. A focus on grace helps us recognize that all people have sinned and stand in need of God's forgiveness and acceptance. Then we no longer sec ourselves as "good people" who are in special favor with God. We approach God humbly and out of our own desperate need.

There are two popular views of sin within the Christian community. The first views sin as breaking one of the rules or laws of the Bible or of the Christian tradition. From that perspective, we are all guilty of sin, because it is impossible for us to fully obey all the rules and laws that are contained in Scripture or that have been developed through the years within the church. Do you gossip? Do you do work of any kind on the Sabbath? Do you find yourself guilty of pride, of feeling superior to others? Do you desire or covet something which belongs to your neighbor?

The second views sin as those actions or even those thoughts which separate us from God, from others, and from what God intended us to become. This is a broader view of sin because it is not the same as a scorecard on rules and laws violated. From this perspective, whatever we do that separates us from God constitutes sin. There may be things we do or even ways in which we think that become barriers to God or to what God would have us do with our lives. Our poor relationships with other people also harm our relationship with God, whether or not we are breaking a specific commandment. Inner thoughts can at times separate us from God just as fully as our outer actions.

Some sins may be more socially acceptable than others, but all sins separate us from God and from the best which God has called us to be. The sins of those who are addicted to alcohol and other drugs may be more visible and less socially acceptable than the sins of pride, greed, and judgmentalism. But there are no grades of sin, making one sin less offensive to God than another. There is no tally of sin with those committing less sin better than those who have committed more. *[A]ll have sinned and fall short of the glory of God"* (Romans 3:23).

It's easy for those of us in the church to develop an attitude of "works righteousness"–the view that we must be right with God because we are doing so many things for the church. But serving on a church board, being a deacon, attending church, tithing, or even being a pastor do not of themselves make us right with God. We are put right with God through God's gracious forgiveness and acceptance of us. When we adopt a religious attitude that is performance oriented, we fall into the trap of relying on our own strength rather than on God's strength.

The emphasis in our contemporary culture on financial success and the satisfaction of material needs draws us toward a works righteousness. We work hard and expect significant financial rewards in the secular world, and it's not surprising that we feel spiritual rewards can be earned in the same way. Christian Community, the research and program development organization of which Steve Clapp is president, conducted a major study on the relationship between the spiritual life and stewardship called the Spirituality and Giving Project. People who were surveyed in congregations across North America acknowledged that they spend considerable time and energy worrying about money and possessions.

Over 90% of those surveyed, all of whom are church active, said that anxiety about money or possessions was one of their top five concerns in life. Over 82% said that it was "very important" to them to earn more money than they currently were. When persons between the ages of 25 and 40 were asked in that study if they would move across the country for a 20% increase in pay, 63% said that they would. When asked if they would work an additional 15 hours a week for a 50% increase in pay, almost all of the respondents except female parents of young children said that they would. The following chart shows the information in graphic form.

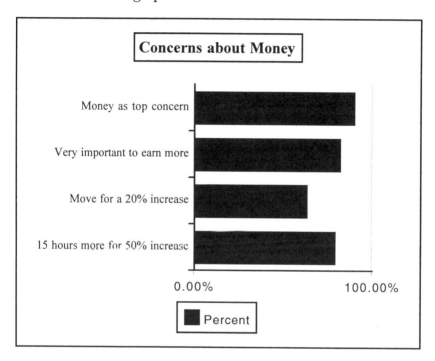

We are in many respects a financially driven and work driven culture. Most of us are willing to work hard, but we expect to be well compensated for it–and we are deeply frustrated if we are not. While those in their twenties and thirties are less likely to be willing to work sixty hour weeks than those in their forties and fifties, younger survey respondents consistently showed a greater concern than older respondents about the importance of making money and being well rewarded for their efforts.

Amy had worked hard to put herself through college, and then she put her husband through graduate school. All along, she assumed that they would have a significant jump in their financial well-being when her husband started working full-time with the advanced degree. To her frustration, he took a position on a university faculty rather than a higher paying industry job. They were doing well but not nearly as well as she had hoped. When she had the opportunity for a significantly higher paying job on the other side of the country, she decided to accept it. At first they talked about maintaining a long distance marriage, but in two years they divorced.

She became more and more aggressive in her climb within the company which had hired her. Amy worked seventy and eighty hour weeks and advanced quickly. When her father died, she, an only child, returned for the funeral but stayed only a day with her mother. When her mother was hospitalized the next year with a heart attack, Amy kept talking to her and the physicians by phone; but she did not feel that she could take the time to travel home and spend time with her mother.

Her mother was scheduled for bypass surgery, and Amy decided to return home the day after the surgery and stay for a long weekend. But her mother died on the operating table, and Amy's return was for the funeral. As she stood by herself at her mother's grave, Amy realized that she had given up everything that was important to her for vocational and financial success. She felt impoverished.

Addiction comes in many forms–none more socially acceptable than addictions to work and to money. When the pursuit of wealth drives so much of what we do, it's easy to begin thinking about all rewards as being the result of our own efforts. Thus being right with God and being a good Christian person can become synonymous in our minds with working hard in the life of the church. While there are certainly rich rewards to expressing our commitment to God through work in the church, that work never brings us new life. That only comes through God's grace.

Grace: More Than a One Time Experience

Like salvation and recovery, grace is more than a one-time experience. Life becomes an adventure in which we continually rediscover the wonder of God's grace and acceptance. Grace gives us the strength to take life a day at a time, to do the right thing when it is difficult, and to accept ourselves and others when we fail. Grace only comes to us when we accept and embrace our weakness, brokenness, and sin. We must discard all of our ego-based pride, self-confidence, and need to be in control. In *Go Away, Come Closer*, Terry Hershey writes: "We must accept the fact that we are incomplete people in a broken world, and none of us can make it alone" [p. 131]. Only in the confession of our weakness and need can the power of grace become real in our lives.

Too often we fall into the trap of comparing ourselves with others. It's easy to say, "Yes, I sin, but I'm not a thief or a murderer, like those people in prison." We think because our sins are fewer in number or more socially acceptable, we are more acceptable to God. Nothing could be further from the truth. The only difference between a casual sinner and an habitual, antisocial sinner is the extent to which grace can impact his or her life. *Where sin increased, grace abounded all the more* (Romans 5:20b).

There is an easy diagnostic test to indicate if we have fully experienced the fullness of God's grace. The test is simple: Are you ever haunted by guilt, shame, or self-doubt about anything? If there is even a hint of those feelings, we have not fully availed ourselves of all that God's grace can do for us. In reality, very few of us have no unresolved guilt, shame, or self-doubt! We may choose not to display those feelings to others and show outward confidence or even self-righteousness. But these attitudes are only masks keeping us from dealing with our sins, weakness, and brokenness. And as long as we keep running away from them, we can never fully experience the gift of grace.

Guilt and shame are not the same thing. Guilt says, *what I did was bad*, while shame says, *I am bad because of all the things I do wrong*. Guilt provides a foundation for humble repentance. In contrast, shame is still self-centered and also self-defeating. Some have suggested that shame is really inverted pride.

Many of us avoid dealing with our guilt because we have transformed it into shame, and the burden of shame can be crippling to us. None of us like to see ourselves as "bad" people. But feeling shame can lead to depression and can make change and renewal seem pointless. If we understand and experience God's grace, we realize that we are not "bad people." We are simply God's children who have strayed and done "bad things."

Our sins can be forgiven, and we can be redeemed. God never stops loving us and seeking to help us. We are all the precious children of God.

One of the signs that we have not fully experienced God's grace is that we sometimes accept God's forgiveness but remain unable to forgive ourselves. We continue to carry the burdens even though God has completely lifted them. We continue to punish and doubt ourselves, even though our sins have been entirely forgiven. This, in many respects, seems like an ego-centered problem. It is as though we erroneously believe that we know more than God. We believe that even though the Almighty God, Ruler of all the universe has forgiven us, we are still justified in not forgiving ourselves. We hold onto our sins like a security blanket even though God let go of them long ago. In fact it may be very difficult for some of us to fully accept the reality that God so willingly forgives our sins.

A Moral Inventory

Taking what 12-step groups call "a searching and fearless moral inventory of ourselves" can play an important role in coming to experience God's forgiveness and grace. This process can be an emotionally heavy one because, by its nature, it focuses somewhat more on our weaknesses than on our strengths. This works best when we actually write the concerns down on paper. The act of writing them down makes us more honest with ourselves and less likely to overlook areas of concern. Here are some of the things such an inventory should include:

- Everything you have done to cause you guilt or shame.

- Every unhealthy fear you have and the source or root of that fear.

- Every resentment and the part we played in broken relationships.

- Every example of putting pleasure above principle in your life. This may include sexual transgressions but can include other areas as well.

- Any other bad habits or characteristics which do not fit in the preceding categories.

- All of the strengths and abilities God has given you.

- All of the positive relationships with others which you have in your life.

- All of the times in the past you have made a positive difference in the lives of others.

- All of the opportunities you are likely to have in the future to make a positive difference in the lives of others.

Such an inventory is not complete until we affirm our good qualities as well as our bad ones. The purpose of this inventory is not to punish or humiliate ourselves but to take an honest look. When we only identify the bad and not the good, we cannot fully experience God's love and grace.

Simply naming our areas of failure is not enough. As a matter of fact, their burden may be even greater than before if we don't actually deal with it. In order to receive and accept God's forgiveness, we need to confess our sins. Confession enables us to get them out in the open and let go of them. Confession allows us to surrender all of our sins, weakness, and brokenness to God instead of struggling with them alone. While we do not have the power to overcome these things ourselves, God has the power, by his grace, to conquer them. We need to fully experience God's grace by surrendering these things to him.

Twelve-step programs suggest that our confession of sin needs to go in three directions: (1) to God, (2) to ourselves, and (3) to another human being. Writing down the moral inventory can become an act of confession to ourselves, and we can then bring those concerns to God in prayer. The Bible also tells us that confession to another is part of the path to healing: *Confess your sins to one another, and pray for one another, so that you may be healed* [James 5:16]. Most of us need to find another human being who is safe, trustworthy, and accepting.

This final aspect of confession sounds frightening because we are making ourselves so vulnerable before another person. Telling everything to another person, however, can result in a huge burden being lifted from one's heart and mind. God's grace and healing suddenly became real through the acceptance of the other person. And because we continue to wrestle with sin and brokenness, confession must be an ongoing process. Starting a relationship with another person to whom we are comfortable confessing can help us on a continuing basis. It's often possible to establish a mutual confessional, sharing relationship with another person which extends over a long period of time.

Fully experiencing God's grace changes the way we relate to those who have hurt us. When we consider all that we have been forgiven, it becomes much easier to forgive others. We are able to let go of resentments and grudges we have harbored for years. Sam shares this experience from his own life:

When I worked as a counselor, I constantly had a personality clash with one of the other counselors in the office named Sharon. One night I had reached my limit with her, so I took my anger and resentment to God. I began listing all of the things she had done to hurt me. I finally concluded, "God, how can you ever forgive someone like that?"

Softly, God answered in the silence of my mind, "Have you ever done any of those things you are angry at Sharon about? Have I forgiven you for those sins? Is there any reason why both you and I shouldn't forgive her?" I quickly inventoried each of Sharon's sins which I had listed. Without exception, I had committed all of these sins myself. I was humbled. But I still didn't like Sharon. God told me that I didn't have to like her, but I had to love her. I had to love her with the same love God had for me—a grace-filled, forgiving love.

A few days later, Sharon and I were riding together in the car after presenting a workshop. Sharon said something that provoked a strong reaction in me, and I was ready for a fight. But I remembered my conversation with God and kept myself from saying all the caustic things I wanted to ventilate. I didn't like her, but I had to love her. So I asked her about her husband, who had been having health problems. I asked about many other things in her life and tried to listen caringly to everything she shared with me. It changed how we related to each other. A few months later when Sharon left that counseling center, she told me that I was one of her best friends.

Fully experiencing God's grace also affects our witness and the witness of the church. We discover that grace is such good news that we want to share it with others. We no longer look down on those outside the church because we know that they are fundamentally no different from us. They need God's grace just as we do, and we want them to experience it.

This new understanding of grace frees the church from its fortress mentality. The church is no longer a fortress defending itself from a terrible and sinful world. Instead, the church becomes a hospital inviting all those who are sick and broken by sin. Obstacles that used to keep people out of church are torn down. All are welcomed, all receive the church's ministry, and all become part of the church's ministry.

In congregational studies across North America, Christian Community has asked over 250,000 active church members to indicate their level of agreement with these statements:

- "A single parent can find welcome and acceptance in our congregation."

- "A person who is struggling with a problem such as alcoholism or other drug addiction can find welcome and acceptance in our congregation."

In congregations which are growing in membership and average attendance, it's not uncommon for over 90% of those surveyed to agree with both statements. In churches which are declining in membership and average attendance, it's not unusual for less than 25% of those surveyed to agree with those statements. In general, people feel that their congregations are somewhat more open to single parents than to persons struggling with alcoholism or other drug addiction.

Those statistical results don't necessarily mean that growing churches owe their success to larger numbers of single parents and persons with drug problems, though those churches are certainly more likely to have such persons as members. What those statistical results suggest is that churches which have a healthy hospitality and a good understanding of God's grace are more open to people of *all kinds of backgrounds*. People can experience acceptance and grace through their interaction with others in those congregations. Members of those churches are more likely to invite others to participate, and visitors are more likely to experience a warm welcome and to want to return. Nothing is more amazing than God's grace.

Nothing is more powerful in ability to transform the lives of people. If we are open and allow it, grace will completely renew us. Grace will heal our broken relationships. And grace will give us a passion for ministry to a broken world.

Chapter Four

The Need for Safe Fellowship

> *Bear one another's burdens, and in this way you will fulfill the law of Christ.*   Galatians 6:2

Sam describes his own recovery experience: *I have been a pastor for over 20 years, and have been in recovery for over 22 years. I have multiple addictions–chemical, relational, and life-style. It is not easy to be a pastor in recovery. When church members learn of the "darker" side of my life, I receive varied responses. One woman thought my recovery would enable me to relate to the youth better. Another man concluded that I was a "sick" person and not qualified to be a pastor.*

By nature, I have difficulty trusting others. Because of the negative responses I sometimes receive, I hesitate to tell churches about my addiction and recovery. In one church I pastored, I didn't tell anyone about my addictions when I first met with them. As my time there progressed, I told a few people in the church on a "need to know" basis. But after 18 months, I prayerfully concluded that it was time to become open about my addiction and recovery.

It was a meaningful day in the church. We had already heard a moving testimony from a woman who accepted Christ while being in prison for murder. God led the soloist to appropriately sing "The Touch of the Master's Hand." I preached on the parable of the Pharisee and the tax collector praying in the Temple (Luke 18:9-14). To illustrate the place of the sinner in the kingdom, I told my story.

Although I was raised in the church and made a commitment to Christ at age 10, I drifted away when I went to college. I was tired of the controlling voices of family and religion telling me who I was supposed to be, so I rebelled. In the course of nine years, I broke nine out of the Ten Commandments. I got involved in street drugs, excessive drinking, and very sick relationships. I tried to counter this behavior by periodic workaholism, but I always regressed to addictive indulgences.

I had acknowledged that I was an addict in 1975, but I rationalized that I didn't need that "12 step stuff." After all, I had a master's degree in clinical psychology and was considered to be one of the best alcohol and drug counselors around. Twelve step recovery was fine for my clients, but I was above that. I was too smart and had my life together. Or so I thought.

I hit bottom in late summer of 1978 while I was working as a counselor in a community mental health center. Not only did I badly betray someone who trusted me, but I also went through the most severe withdrawal from my addiction that I had ever experienced. I was unable to sleep or eat for two weeks, and I was constantly shaking.

As if I a veil had been lifted, I began to look at my life honestly for the first time. Like the prodigal son, I came to myself (Luke 15:17). Loneliness had always been the demon that haunted me most deeply. I was unable to maintain a healthy relationship with anyone because of my addiction. Hopeful relationships always ended the same way: either I hurt the other person deeply or I was rejected and left alone. No matter what I did or how smart or educated I was, I would be alone for the rest of my life. My intelligence and knowledge had not saved me from addiction, but only enabled me to develop more complicated denial systems. There was no hope for me to ever live the life of happiness I envisioned.

I began to contemplate suicide. As usual, I began to think of ending my life in the way that was least painful to me. I had no thought or care for how my suicide would affect my family or friends around me. I simply wanted out. I wanted the inward pain, emptiness, and craving to be gone once and for all.

As I pondered methods of suicide, a still small voice spoke to my heart: "Sam, what do you tell clients who are in your position?" The answer was simple: "I tell them to work the 12 steps of recovery." The voice responded: "Why don't you try them?"

*For the first time, I was humbled enough to consider this, so I began Step 1: **"We admitted we were powerless over our addiction and that our lives had become unmanageable."***

This was an easy step because it described where I was perfectly. My life was totally out of control, and I was powerless to change it.

Step 2: "Came to believe that a Power greater than ourselves could restore us to sanity." While I had turned my back on the church, I still believed in God. I mostly ignored him, although I called on him occasionally when I wanted something. I wasn't sure if God could or would help me. But if he failed me, I could always revert to my suicide option.

Step 3: "Made a decision to turn our will and our lives over to the care of God." I humbly and prayerfully surrendered my life to him. Nothing dynamic happened. There were no emotional explosions or feelings of ecstasy. But the emptiness in my heart began to evaporate, and I felt a fullness I had never experienced before. The constant anxiety and shakes quietly ended, and I felt an inner peace.

My recovery began in earnest. I shared this with my work supervisor, who happened to be an ordained minister. Before I knew it, I was serving as a lay speaker in a local church. Then my career shifted, and I entered pastoral ministry. Although this process began in October of 1978, recovery continues to be an ongoing process and my main avenue for growing in my relationship with God and his people.

As I shared this story with my congregation during the message, tears began to appear on the cheeks of many of those attending. I offered an altar call during the last hymn. The dam broke when the pianist, unable to control her weeping, came up to embrace me. Many others followed. A quiet farmer told me that he was glad I was his pastor.

For the first time ever, I felt safe sharing my addiction and recovery with a faith community. In my experience, Christians had often proved untrustworthy, but finally there was acceptance, encouragement, and love. At that moment, I experienced the safe fellowship that the church was supposed to be.

There are many other addictions, problems, and conditions which people are uncomfortable sharing unless they feel in a safe fellowship. For example, while we especially associate eating disorders with young people, the reality is that these problems threaten the overall physical, mental, emotional, and spiritual lives of people of all ages. As shared in Chapter Two, the U.S. Department of Health and Human Services estimates that over five million adolescent girls and women struggle with eating disorders; over one million boys and men also struggle with these diseases. Many feel total isolation because eating disorders are so alienating and shameful. It is also a disease that even very close friends and family are afraid to bring up to the one suffering.

In addition, half of American women and one-quarter of men arc on a diet any given day. Popular images of what constitutes being attractive have a powerful impact on people. Americans spend over $40 billion on dieting and diet-related products each year (U.S. Department of Health and Human Services). Some persons with addictive eating disorders will never find success through a traditional dieting program.

There are many addiction problems that people may struggle with alone but which may also seriously affect others in the process. For example:

- Alcoholism
- Excessive Anger and Violence
- Drug Addiction/Abuse (including cigarette smoking)
- Sex Addiction
- Excessive Fears and Worries
- Erratic Behaviors that Harm Self and Others
- Depression and Suicidal Thoughts
- Excessive Self-Indulgence

The Safety of Church Fellowship

Churches vary in how safe they are. Some churches are very safe, providing acceptance, healing, and sanctuary to broken people. Other churches, however, are very unsafe, offering only condemnation, judgment, and religious guilt trips to those who are broken. Most churches vacillate between these two extremes. Sometimes they are safe and sometimes they are not. Where the church happens to be depends on the vision of the membership and the vigilance of the church leaders.

It is no small thing that the very first word of the first step in recovery is "we." Recovery is a "we" thing and not a "me" thing. Safe, loving, and healing fellowship is indispensable. Recovery comes through relationships–with God, with self, and with others.

Yet the church has too often succumbed to one of the worst possible heresies: "God and me, but I don't need thee!" Believers are encouraged to have their own private, personal relationship with God through Jesus Christ. But relationship with other believers is often underemphasized and regarded as optional. Second Corinthians 5:17 says that we need to be "in Christ." But how can we be in Christ if we neglect to be in the body of Christ?

Terry Hershey tells us of the danger of this heresy in *Go Away, Come Back*: "In the church, we have fanned the flame of this rugged individualism by advocating a 'just me and Jesus' theology" [p.132]. Our faith is incomplete without deep, safe relationships with other believers. Close spiritual connections with people and close spiritual connections with God are interrelated. A detached intellectual search for religious truth can leave us empty if we are not meaningfully connected with others.

Fellowship is basic to our faith. We are called to bear one another's burdens. We are not called to ignore, condemn, or gossip about them. We are called to bear them. And this way, we *"fulfill the law of Christ"* (Galatians 6:2).

In safe relationships we deal directly with people. We are honest with people about our feelings, concerns, and needs. In Christian maturity, we have learned to *"speak. . . the truth in love"* (Ephesians 4:15). Truth without love is harsh and cruel. Love without truth is codependent and enabling. Truth and love must go hand in hand in all of our relationships.

Hazards to a Loving Christian Fellowship

Triangulation can destroy relationships. This occurs when we share our honest concerns with someone other than the person directly involved in the situation. In essence, triangulation is another word for gossip, which is the number one killer of safe fellowship. Gossip destroys relationships and damages fellowship in several ways:

47

First, it often involves character assassination. In the Sermon on the Mount, Jesus takes the commandment against murder and gives it a broader interpretation:

> *You have heard that it was said to those of ancient*
> *times, "You shall not murder"; and whoever murders*
> *shall be liable to judgment. But I say to you that if you*
> *are angry with a brother or sister, you will be liable*
> *to judgment; and if you insult a brother or sister, you*
> *will be liable to the council; and if you say, "You fool,"*
> *you will be liable to the hell of fire.* [Matthew 5:21-22]

We need to be very careful what we say to other persons and what we say about other persons. The Letter of James reminds us of the power and danger of gossip and of the tongue:

> *For every species of beast and bird, of reptile and*
> *sea creature, can be tamed and has been tamed*
> *by the human species, but no one can tame the tongue*
> *–a restless evil, full of deadly poison. With it we*
> *bless the Lord and Father, and with it we curse those*
> *who are made in the likeness of God. From the*
> *same mouth come blessing and cursing. My brothers*
> *and sisters, this ought not to be so.* [James 3:7-10]

Second, gossip often makes assumptions about the person who is being discussed. While some of these assumptions may be true, they are often extended into exaggerations and outright lies. The only way to deal with assumptions that are both true and untrue is to go directly to the person involved. Many misperceptions can be corrected by direct communication.

When Sam worked in a psychiatric unit in Kansas City, some of the staff would engage in "gossip" about the patients. They would hide their maliciousness behind clinical observations and psychological jargon. Whenever Sam heard this gossip, he decided to check out its validity. He addressed this issue with patients, asking: "Have you ever considered that you are actually doing this with your behavior?" Sometimes, patients denied it. But usually, they thought about it and thanked him for a valuable insight into their problems. Staff could have been more helpful by talking directly with patients rather than with others about them.

Third, gossip harms those who engage in it. Whenever we gossip, we are usually judging others. And when we judge others, we are opening ourselves up to judgment. Jesus said: *"Do not judge, so that you may not be judged"* (Matthew 7:1).

Gossip harms us by taking our focus away from our own sins and character defects. When we talk about others, we are generally powerless to change them, even if we are correct in our observations. But most of all, we avoid self-honesty by focusing on the sins and character defects of others. While we cannot change them, we can change ourselves with God's help. Taking our own moral inventory produces healthier relationships with others in the end.

Finally, gossip destroys the safe fellowship of the church. Many people will not share their hurt, brokenness, or sin with other Christians because of gossip. They do not want their problems to be talked about or exaggerated in future conversations with others. But if the church provides an open and nonjudgmental welcome to people, allowing them to freely express their hurt, the church can become one of the most safe, healing places for broken people.

The Healing Church

Jesus clearly called the church to be a safe, healing community. One of the most basic human desires is to be in relationships with others. These relationships bring meaning and fullness to life. Real intimacy is achieved when two or more people share their own pain and suffering with others without an atmosphere of fear and intimidation. When this is realized, one can experience pure joy and nourishment of the soul.

People who avoid intimacy do so because they have been hurt in the past by others they wanted to trust. Therefore, we cannot simply write off people who are afraid of intimate fellowship in their faith walk. We need to patiently understand those who are shy and untrusting as we accept their pain and encourage their healing. Only then will they be able to trust again.

We should provide a true atmosphere of love and safety in the church. Twelve step programs have done this, and so must the church. But how? There are two concrete ways to fulfill this need.

First, we can encourage people, especially new believers, to form partnerships with spiritual mentors or directors. Twelve step programs call this person a "sponsor." In this sponsorship, a person is matched with a more spiritually mature person to help them with their brokenness and growth. The person new to the program often talks with his or her mentor regularly by telephone and direct contact.

As their relationship builds, the new member shares more of his or her sins, struggles, hopes, and dreams with the mentor. The mentor is required to be a good listener who is nonjudgmental and accepting. The mentor is not an advice-giver but someone who reflects reality back to the new member by sharing his or her own experience, strength, and hope. The confession recommended in the last chapter could well be done with a mentor or sponsor. For obvious reasons, it is best if men have male mentors and women have female mentors.

As new members grow in their healing and faith, they too will reach a point when they can mentor others. Thus, the tradition of safe relationships is received and passed on to others who desperately need it. In this way, the reality of safe fellowship grows in the faith community.

Second, churches can provide safe fellowship through small groups. These small groups can be Sunday School classes or Bible study groups. Groups work best in providing safe fellowship when they are based on common need. Churches can offer small groups for various needs: overeaters, parents of teenagers, parents of young children, single parents, recovering alcoholics, childhood abuse victims, people who have lost a spouse, people seeking to grow in the spiritual life, and more. These small groups produce the greatest intimacy when the importance of confidentiality is continually stressed to participants.

To begin such groups, church leadership should secure the lay leadership of a spiritually mature member of the church who shares that struggle and need. They should be encouraged and provided with resources to successfully make that group happen. Many Bible study resources can help structure these groups and make them a safe environment for sharing our experience, strength, and hope. Some of these resources will be discussed in the last chapter.

Third, churches should be both positive and realistic if they utilize a sharing time in worship. Some churches have a time in worship known as "joys and concerns" during which members and visitors can share significant experiences in their lives and request the prayers of the congregation. These are often rich opportunities which help build a sense of supportive community in the congregation as a whole. People will often share good news like the birth of a child, an engagement, or recovery from an illness. They may ask for prayers because of a coming surgery, the loss of a loved one, or a major decision which is faced. In some congregations, the scope of joys and concerns is broadened to include events in the community and the world–people may request prayers for the hungry, for peace in the Middle East, or for assistance in an alcoholic treatment center. The joys and concerns concept works best when these guidelines are remembered:

- This should not be a time for announcements about church or community events. In fact, if there is going to be enough time for joys and concerns, it is usually important for the announcements to be printed in the bulletin.

- Those who are sharing should be instructed, perhaps through wording in the bulletin or program, to give their names so that others know who is talking. This kind of sharing is not like the anonymous sharing of an A.A. meeting. People in the church seek to know one another, and those who do not know a speaker will feel left out.

- Church leaders need to set the example of doing the sharing in such a way that those listening can understand what is being discussed. Speakers, especially in small congregations, sometimes assume that everyone knows the context of which they are speaking. Someone may say: "My father is back in the hospital again. He needs prayers and cards." That kind of sharing assumes that everyone knows the name of the person's father and the hospital.

51

- Church leaders also need to model a style of sharing which is clear but also short. If people use the joys and concerns time to offer their own mini-sermons, the service will be too long and the sharing will be unappreciated.

In larger congregations, time may not make a "joys and concerns" realistic. Many churches have developed systems of prayer request cards which can help meet some of the same need. The prayer requests can be collected and given to the pastor, who can share a few requests as part of the morning prayer. Requests can also be shared through the bulletin and the newsletter.

It's important to be aware that there are limitations on the joys and concerns concept. Except in very small congregations, few people are going to be comfortable sharing concerns of a sensitive or potentially embarrassing nature with the whole church. Someone is not likely to say to the whole gathered congregation "I have a drinking problem" or "Our daughter is too sexually active for a person her age, and we don't know what to do." Small group settings, with an expectation of confidentiality, feel much safer for that kind of sharing.

Fourth, pastors and other leaders in the church can model a refusal to engage in gossip or in pointless criticism of others. Gossip can be like an infectious disease, which spreads from person to person and group to group, seemingly out of control. Pastors, other staff, volunteer teachers, and elected leaders of the church are in positions to help reduce the amount of gossip and criticism which becomes part of church life. Those reading this book are likely to have opportunities to help in this area.

Suppose, for example, that someone says, "I heard that Tom Watson lost his job because he was suspected of embezzling money from the company." Rather than accepting that statement at face value and then passing it on to others, consider responding in words similar to these: "I certainly don't know if that is true or not, but that rumor could sure be destructive to Tom and his family. Let's do what we can to keep it from spreading."

Or suppose someone says, "I think Susan Molinaro is doing a pathetic job as property chairperson. She hasn't done anything about the chipped paint in the classrooms, and I've never seen the church kitchen as dirty as it has been this fall." Rather than simply accepting that statement and passing it on to others, consider saying something like: "I know that Susan and her husband spend a lot of time working for the church. I wonder if she's getting the help she needs from the others on the property committee. I wouldn't want her to think she was the subject of gossip. Maybe we should visit with her about the concern."

Fifth, pastors can use sermons as opportunities to encourage the creation of safe fellowship in the church and to point out the harm which is done by gossip. People in fact are hungry for safe fellowship, for being in a community of people who are continually encouraging and supportive rather than gossiping and hurtful. Our human tendency to talk about others without considering the consequences, however, works against the creation of that kind of community. The pastor has opportunity through sermons to build a biblical foundation for the creation of safe fellowship and to help members and constituents better understand the harm done by gossip.

Lessons Learned . . .

At the present time in his recovery journey, Sam sometimes feels more safe with some Christians and less safe with others. In contrast, he almost always feels safe in the 12-step recovery group. Christ intended the church to be a secure place–a sanctuary. It is time we make our faith communities into safe fellowships.

In congregational surveys around North America, Christian Community has consistently found that growing churches are far more likely than declining churches to have a large percentage of members and constituents (persons who are involved in the congregation but are not members) agreeing that:

- There are persons in this church with whom I am comfortable sharing my deepest thoughts and concerns.

- You can share differences of opinion in this church without being put down by others.

- I feel cared about in this church in a deeper way than I have experienced in other organizations.

The church at its best is a safe place, where differences of opinion and diversity in membership are respected. Members and constituents can be themselves and express their beliefs and feelings without fear of becoming objects of gossip.

Chapter Five
The Need for Integrity

> "Let your words be 'Yes, Yes' or 'No, No';
> anything more than this comes from the
> evil one."   Matthew 5:37, NRSV

Roger recovered from being a "low bottom" drunk where he nearly reached the point of sleeping under bridges. He went through two unsuccessful marriages that failed as a direct result of his drinking. He was arrested over 60 times for public intoxication and driving while under the influence. His driver's license was revoked for life.

Roger reached a turning point. He got off the bottle and eventually celebrated 18 years of sobriety. He was considered one of the "good, old timers" at AA meetings. When he spoke, people listened. He had a spiritual depth and maturity that few ever achieve. He journeyed from a cynical agnosticism to a faith in a Higher Power to trust in Jesus Christ as his Lord and Savior. He was baptized and became a respected member of his church.

But not all was well. He drove to church. He drove to AA meetings. He drove to work. Because he had no driver's license, Roger drove with one he borrowed from a relative. He saw little hope of ever getting his license back, so he believed driving illegally was his best alternative. Roger recognized this lack of integrity in his recovery, and his illegal driving haunted him. One night while driving he prayed: "God, help me make this right." Evidently, while he was praying, he failed to dim his brights for an oncoming car. The car made a U-turn and followed him. Police lights appeared in his rear view mirror. He was caught. Because he knew this was God's answer to prayer, he profusely thanked the astonished policeman for arresting him. Nevertheless, he spent the night in the county jail.

Upon his release, Roger had difficulty finding an attorney to represent him. He was considered an habitual offender, and his case was not promising. His 18 years of successful sobriety and his strong Christian faith counted for nothing in the eyes of the court. Finally, he found a lawyer who would take his case. Using a technicality he found in one of Roger's driving arrests, the lawyer was able to get his driver's license back, and Roger started driving legally again. He was overwhelmed with thanksgiving to God for answering his prayer. His integrity was intact.

Today Roger is driving a delivery truck. He is going to school at night and beginning a ministry to prison inmates who are returning to the community. He is living his life with integrity before God and before the state license bureau. Roger is at peace again.

The Dilemma of Honesty and Integrity

Integrity is a deceptive virtue that we constantly search for. We like to think of ourselves as honest people, and for the most part we are. But dishonesty still haunts us. Perhaps we tell white lies to make others feel better or to help our own cause. Perhaps, like Roger, we have behaviors in our lives that are truly inconsistent with our value system. We may "fudge" on tax returns or habitually watch television shows with viewpoints that may directly conflict with our value system. Perhaps we exude love and compassion in our homes and churches but become cutthroats at work. Perhaps we cheer for family values but find ourselves too busy to spend time with our own families.

It is distressing to recognize how common lying and cheating have become in our society. According to a survey conducted by *Who's Who Among American High School Students* in 2000, 80 percent of high-achieving high school students admitted they had cheated; 50 percent of them said they did not necessarily think it was wrong; and 95 percent of them said they had never been caught in the act.

It is often easy for us to assume that only those in compromising careers and positions fall prey to living lives filled with deceit. *U.S. News* polled roughly a thousand adults in 1999, asking who they thought were most likely to cheat others. The following people are thought of, from highest to lowest rank, as cheating most often (Do these answers surprise you?):

- Politicians– 89%
- Lawyers - 78%
- Journalists and the media - 76%
- CEOs of Fortune 500 companies - 73%
- Government employees - 72%
- Rich people - 69%
- IRS agents - 55%
- Poor people - 45%
- Doctors - 40%

What does cheating mean? The *U.S. News* study found that the common forms of cheating are having extramarital sex; taking credit for other people's work; recording extra hours on a time sheet; earning money and not paying taxes on it; taking work supplies for home use; writing false information on a resume; keeping incorrect change from a cashier; and saying that payment is in the mail when it isn't.

Jesus spoke of integrity in the Sermon on the Mount when he said our "yes" should mean "yes" and our "no" should mean "no." At face value, this seems like a directive to be honest that we can easily follow. Some denominations take this as a clear indication that, when we are in a legal setting, we should not take oaths but only affirm to tell the truth. While this approach may appear somewhat legalistic, these Christians understand a deeper truth.

If we swear we are telling the truth, then that implies that we are free to lie when we are not under oath. We can live as people of integrity on Sunday, but let our behavior go in real life situations. We play "King's X." In this childhood game, we were free not to tell the truth when we had our fingers crossed behind our backs. How many times do we mentally cross our fingers behind our backs?

This teaching of Jesus also says we need to tell the simple truth. Nothing more and nothing less. Too often we over-explain things in order to bury the truth under a flood of words. Perhaps the listener will get lost in the words and not hear the truth we don't want known. Or perhaps we embellish stories to make us look good. We disguise the truth behind excuses, rationalizations, blaming, and meager attempts to elicit sympathy from the listener.

Living with integrity is one of our greatest challenges. It's difficult because integrity is tested daily in seemingly small ways. Sam once worked in the admissions office of a college where he was asked to mail some college promotional materials to one of the representatives in the field. He procrastinated endlessly and was finally reduced to asking the college president to deliver it as he made a business trip to the same area.

The president asked, "Sam, why wasn't this material sent out previously like it was supposed to be?" Sam's mind raced through all kinds of rationalizations, excuses and elaborate stories to defend himself. But his conscience convicted him of the dishonesty. So his reply was, "I have no excuse. I should have done it before. Please forgive me."

Our integrity often fails because we don't want to seem bad to anyone. We want to impress others, and we want everyone to like us. We focus on our assets and neglect to tell people about our relevant character defects. We are not being honest with them, and inevitably, we are not being honest with ourselves. We want others to feel good about us and we about ourselves, so we continue to hide our "dark side."

But God knows better. And it haunts us that God knows all these things. Therefore, we put on a mask of religious behavior hoping God won't see. Then we cringe when we hear the words of the psalmist: *O Lord, You have searched me and You know me* (Psalm 139:1).

The promise of Jesus scares us: *"There is nothing concealed that will not be disclosed, or hidden that will not be made known. What you have said in the dark will be heard in the daylight, and what you have whispered in the ear in the inner rooms will be proclaimed from the roofs"* (Luke 12:2-3). According to this gospel, all of our sins, character defects, shortcomings, and bad habits will eventually be revealed to everyone! Not only will God know, but so will everyone else.

Every week, we may put on our Sunday best and present smiling, friendly faces to everyone with whom we worship. We may act like everything is well with our lives, and we may pretend that we have it all together. We may tell no one of the angry fight we had with our spouse the night before. We may hope no one has heard that our teenage son is struggling with drug abuse. We may never confess that an uncle was arrested for embezzling funds from his company. Our outwardly religious behavior is a thin covering for deep pain.

As discussed in the last chapter, the church at its best represents a safe place, where we can be open about the pain, suffering, and challenges of life. No matter how safe the community of the church, however, we still must decide whether or not to be open.

The Means of Transforming our Lives

How can we heal if we won't reveal the wounds? How can we live out our faith when we don't live our lives with complete integrity? At this juncture, we need healthy doses of both grace and transformation. The question then becomes: how do we transform ourselves to live a life of integrity? Twelve-step programs have a threefold suggestion for enabling God's transforming power to move in our lives and change us: *honesty, open-mindedness,* and *willingness.* They are often abbreviated in the acronym HOW.

Let us begin with *honesty.* The primary obstacle to honesty is denial, which was discussed earlier. Without honesty, the spiritual foundations of our lives can be destroyed. In *The Secret Life of the Soul,* Keith Miller writes: ". . . at each step of the way toward spiritual growth of the soul there is a chance to take responsibility and grow–or to deny, blame, and stay stuck in bewildering anxiety and stress" (p 18). When we live out of touch with reality, we begin to experience a kind of spiritual disintegration, which eats at the very foundation of our lives.

Honesty is a painful process. We don't want to face the lack of integrity in our lives, but it is far better than living dishonestly before God, self, and others. With this in mind, we can see that honesty is not simply an abstract ideal but a practical way of living. Honesty is most easily accomplished with accountability. It is helpful to have a spiritual sponsor or mentor, as discussed in the previous chapter. Sam will often meet with his sponsor and ramble on as if everything is just great in his life. But his sponsor knows him too well to let him get by with this. He often interrupts Sam and says, "Sam, what's really going on? I can sense something is bothering you." Sam knows he has been caught, and he will then tell his sponsor his real feelings and struggles.

Honesty is also facilitated by an accountability group, which was suggested in the previous chapter as well. Being in a group works two ways. First, it gives us a place where we can safely share what is really going on. This has a cathartic quality allowing us to release hurts, memories, and habitual behaviors that plague our integrity.

Second, the group's honesty will often convict us about our lack of integrity. Often another group member will share how he or she has been dishonest with God, self, and others. In their stories, we begin to see a reflection of ourselves. And in the mirror image that we cannot avoid, we are forced to be honest. While this process sounds frightening, it is not, except for perhaps the first time we are truly honest with our accountability group. There is a true freedom in sharing with caring and accepting people who are struggling with the same issues.

The second aspect of HOW is *open-mindedness*. Open-mindedness is often difficult because we are full of our own opinions about everything. We get so consumed with our own perspective that we often cannot see the truth. We hide behind the self-centered delusion that we are right, and the world would be a better place if everyone saw things our way. Being stuck in our own opinions and perspective makes it impossible for God to change us. God cannot transform self-centered, self-satisfied people. He can only transform humble people who are constantly open to a better way.

Sam once discussed Christian values with a newly converted Christian, asking what his beliefs were about war in light of Jesus' message to love our enemies (Matthew 5:43-47). Sam expected either an argument for pacifism or a defense of the "just war" theory espoused by Martin Luther. Instead, he gave Sam a humble answer filled with open-mindedness: "I am praying and waiting for God to show me what I should believe about war." Sam was left speechless and humbled.

When we are confronted with a truth about ourselves that is difficult to face, we usually respond in one of two very destructive ways. First, we may become highly defensive. We rush to make excuses and rationalize our position. We may even begin to find fault with the person who has been instrumental in confronting us with this truth. We run from the truth because we fear admitting that we are wrong might be the same as confessing that we are bad people.

Nothing could be further from the truth. Whether we are actually right or wrong, we are still loved by God. Our worth is in the love and grace of Jesus Christ, not in our rightness or wrongness.

Our second destructive response when confronted is self-invalidation. Some of us may view every accusation we receive as an excuse to put ourselves down and feel badly about who we are. We may ignore the compliments others give us while taking every criticism to heart. We may often even lack the ability or willingness to differentiate between accurate truths and false accusations. We sometimes needlessly blame and punish ourselves for things we did or did not do.

True open-mindedness weighs every confrontation with self-honesty. When we have open-mindedness, we can discard accusations without disparaging those who accuse us. Others are considered and prayed for. Seldom do we feel badly about ourselves because we know we are precious children of God. We see these truths as opportunities to look honestly at ourselves and thus become better people. We simply open ourselves to God's sanctification process and work with Him on becoming better people with fewer character defects.

As shared before, such open-mindedness is best pursued with safe accountability groups and accepting mentors, so that we know negative feedback is given out of love and regard for our own well-being. We know these people love us in spite of our worst character defects. We can deal with them honestly and safely. And with the help of God and others, we can become all that God intended us to be.

Now consider the final aspect of HOW: *willingness*. To put it simply, we may know the truth about ourselves, but it is worthless unless we are willing to do something about it. God cannot change us unless we are willing to change. In the process of being honest with ourselves, we often discover two truths. We may discover a character defect that keeps us from living in healthier ways. We may also discover that we are truly unwilling to change this shortcoming. We are comfortable with it and not yet ready to give it up.

What do we do at this point? We should not beat ourselves up because we are overly attached to a certain sin or character defect. Instead, we should confess our unwillingness honestly and humbly as we would with any other shortcoming. Then we pray, asking God to give us this willingness. God is truly in every part of the transformation process. He not only gives us the ability to change but also the very desire to change. But these things only will come to us if we humbly ask.

The Continuing Search for Integrity

Integrity is often an elusive ideal. We may think we have achieved it only to discover another aspect of ourselves that is incongruent with whom we want to be. Thus, the search for integrity is an ongoing, lifelong process. While we may never reach a point of complete integrity, we can have integrity about the very process of searching for it. It is a process that will free us from destructive attitudes, beliefs, and actions. And it is a process that will help us truly feel self-worth and experience personal growth.

A church which is committed to doing so has tremendous potential to encourage us in the process of leading lives of greater honesty. This can be accomplished through instruction to children, youth, and adults in Sunday School, worship services, and other settings. Youth groups can play an important role, for example, in helping young people cope with the competitive pressures of school in ways that preserve integrity. They give youth a peer support system that validates Christian decision-making, attitudes, and behaviors. Sunday School is also an opportunity for any age group to learn how to live the kind of life Christ spoke about. Church is the perfect setting to not only instill the values of honesty and integrity in those who worship together but to uphold them in an atmosphere of true love for one another.

Chapter Six
The Need for Freedom

> *and you will know the truth and the truth
> will set you free.*   John 8:32

Sam provides an example from his youth of the dilemma of living with guilt that is unresolved until the truth is told:

When I was about ten or eleven, I loved to camp with my friends in the woods behind our house. We would load up our tents, sleeping bags, and other camping accessories, walk a hundred yards into the woods, and feel like we were in an isolated wilderness. Knowing my love of camping, my parents gave me a beautiful shiny hatchet with a glossy leather handle.

We would often leave our campsite up all summer so we could periodically visit it. One day, after a period of rain, I walked past the campsite only to see my beautiful hatchet unprotected and covered with rust. I was instantly overcome with fear, guilt and shame. What would my parents say to me when they saw that I hadn't taken care of this wonderful gift? I quickly ran home.

I tried not to think about it, but there were remorse-filled moments before going to sleep at night or after waking up in the morning. A few weeks later, I was walking through the woods and happened by the campsite. There it was again: that rusty hatchet reminding me of my guilt and shame. This time I had enough sense to throw a tarp over it to prevent further rusting. But I still held this secret in my heart, afraid to tell anyone of my sin. Several weeks later, I again walked by the campsite. This time I picked up the hatchet and carried it home carefully so no one would see me hide it in the basement. With a summer full of an eleven-year-old's adventures, I didn't have much time to think about it. But occasionally the thoughts would bring back the same guilty feelings.

This went on for several months. But the episodes of terrible feelings in my gut began to lengthen and intensify. After a while, any idle waking moment I had went back to that rusty hatchet and

*how I had disappointed my parents by not caring for their gift. I felt
haunted by those feelings.*

*One morning I woke up in excruciating emotional pain thinking
about my rusty hatchet. I couldn't take it anymore, and I began to
cry. I knew the moment of truth had arrived because I could not go
on the way I had been. I said a short prayer and mustered up what
little courage I had to make a confession to my mother. I went
downstairs crying and muttered, "Mom, I'm so sorry. I ruined that
wonderful hatchet you gave me. I left it out in the rain and it's all
rusty now."*

*To my surprise, not one word of condemnation came out of my
mother's mouth. She reassured and comforted me. She got some
sandpaper from my dad's workshop and began to sand off the rust.
This then became my job, and I sanded every speck of rust.*

*That beautiful hatchet was never shiny again. But it remained
functional for many years and many camping trips. More
importantly though, I had told the truth, and the truth had set me
free.*

Set Free by the Truth

Many of us live in a constant state of spiritual and
psychological oppression, held hostage by shame, resentment,
self-doubt, and other negative attitudes. We need to learn to
treat ourselves with the same grace that God has given us. We
need to stop beating ourselves up for what we aren't, and affirm
ourselves for who we are. We need to celebrate who God has
created us to be.

We don't have to hide our character defects. We don't have
to be afraid that someone might find out about the skeletons in
our closets. We no longer need to minimize and excuse our
secret sins. We need to admit them to ourselves. We need to
present them to God. We need to confess them to others who
are safe and accepting. All this is followed by acceptance,
forgiveness, and grace. And we are free.

But are we free from having them occur again? Character
defects and sins tend to be habitual and addictive. All the

willpower in the world cannot stop them. But God can. God not only forgives our sin, but he also will "cleanse us from all unrighteousness" (1 John 1:9b, NRSV). Not only are the sins of the past taken away, but also the sins of the present and the future.

In *Crooked Little Heart*, Anne Lamott tells the story of a thirteen-year-old named Rosie who begins cheating in tennis. The first time involved almost no thought at all as she called a ball "out" when it was in fact "in." Her body had been positioned in such a way that her opponent did not see where the ball hit, and there were no consequences to the lie. The lie was very easy, and she won a game she would otherwise have lost. The next time it was easier to cheat, and the next time it was even easier. Soon Rosie began to feel good rather than bad about the cheating:

> *God, she thought. You spend all this time trying to do right but always feeling wrong, and you wonder why you never get ahead and why it takes so much energy, like tightrope walking. And then here she was getting away with cheating, and for some reason in that she found a huge relief. She'd stopped being so good, and she no longer worried so much about falling off the tightrope.* [p. 137]

Of course the sense of relief does not last. The cheating begins to eat at Rosie's own confidence and self-esteem even before those who play with her begin to recognize her propensity for altering the truth for her own benefit. She becomes a prisoner of her own selfish actions, and she is emotionally tormented until she confesses what she has done.

Jesus taught us that the truth will set us free. We often ask with Pilate, "What is truth?" (John 18:38, NRSV). And, like Pilate, we sometimes turn away before Jesus can answer us. Or else we diminish and limit the truth. Truth must be experiential. It needs to be both in our heads and our hearts. It needs to be in our thoughts and our behaviors. It needs to be both in our belief systems and in our relationships. Unless God's truth is in all these things, it cannot completely set us free.

Such freedom allows us to become all God intended us to
be. "Freedom is being normal," according to Gilbert Romero,
pastor of the Bella Vista Church of the Brethren, in East Los
Angeles. It means being free around each other, being honest
and accepted. It means not putting on fronts and playing
Christian roles, but being ourselves as God created us to be.

Without this freedom, our soul is imprisoned and trapped.
Almost all of the things that enslave us are "false idols." They
are not made of gold or wood or even money. They are idols of
the mind, heart, and attitude. We lose our freedom when we put
any false attitude or priority before God. What is troublesome is
that some of these idolatrous attitudes are so subtle and
ingrained that we may never realize that they are there. John's
warning is more relevant to us than we think when he wrote,
"Little children, keep away from idols." (1 John 5:21, NRSV)

Alcoholism has been a recurring example in this book to
describe the pain associated with excesses and holding onto
idolatrous thoughts and behaviors. Some of us who are not
alcoholics are trapped by another common addiction of our time:
workaholism. Workaholism causes us to lose freedom because
we are too focused on vocational success and financial gain.
(Chapter Three discussed some of the problems which result
when money becomes too important in our lives.) Some
examples of workaholism and the resulting problems follow.
Perhaps you can identify with one or more of these:

Workaholic #1: *John is a 27-year-old computer programmer who
works for an Internet start-up company in California. He lives with
his parents, but they see very little of him these days. He usually
doesn't get home until sometime between midnight and 3 A.M., and
he is generally asleep when they leave for work. There is a futon in
his office at work, and he sometimes crashes on it to sleep a few
hours before beginning work again. If the company is successful,
he and the others on the ground floor will make a tremendous
amount of money. The result is, however, tremendous pressure to
maintain schedules and work almost all the time. He and his
colleagues have virtually no social life outside of work.*

Workaholic #2: *Wendy is a 45-year-old human resources
executive in a Midwest firm that is going through major changes.
The company is downsizing to increase profitability, so she has to
work with the termination of many employees. At the same time,*

the company is expanding its research and development work, so she is directing recruiting efforts for people with doctorates in highly technical fields. She has experienced the positive effects of downsizing by getting two promotions while those around her were losing their jobs. But the reason for her success is her unwavering commitment to getting the job done, no matter what it takes. Her work day normally starts at 7 A.M., and she rarely leaves for home before 7 P.M.. Many of her recruiting contacts have to be made after 5 P.M. because she is trying to lure people away from other companies, and those people aren't comfortable talking from work.

When she finally comes home, she usually brings a briefcase of materials to review and sometimes a list of three or four phone numbers to call. If she takes Saturday off to spend time with her junior high daughter and her senior high son, then she goes in on Sunday to catch up again. Her husband works a similar pace and is very understanding, but their children experience disappointment over the amount of time their parents are gone. Wendy is happy about the professional and financial success she and her husband have achieved, but she sometimes wonders how they will view these years when they look back on them—or how their children will view them.

Workaholic #3: U.S. News & World Report had a cover story titled "Working Harder than Ever" in the December 20, 1999 issue. The article describes a comptroller of a company who pushed herself to work six weeks without a single day off, generally starting at 5 A.M. and continuing until 10 P.M. to prepare for an initial public offering. She came home at 9 P.M. one evening because her daughter pleaded for help with homework. After they had completed the assignment, her daughter said to her, "Now that I don't have a homework problem, I won't see you again." A new C.E.O. brought some changes to that company, but the typical work week there is still 55 to 65 hours.

Family and friends suffer the effects of the hours put in by workaholics, all because they believe they are doing good for their loved ones by bringing in more material wealth. Those of us who admit to this behavior realize that, in the end, the time we spend with our friends and family is more precious than any money we earn.

Idolatrous Thoughts: The Path to True Unfulfillment

Dan Stewart, of Calvary Chapel in Newport Mesa, California, believes that our society worships four idolatrous attitudes which enslave us and keep us from the freedom that God gave us:

- *I need to feel good all the time.*
- *I need to have everyone like me.*
- *I need to be right all the time.*
- *I need to be in control.*

Let's explore each of these idolatrous thoughts in more detail.

Idolatrous Thought #1: *I need to feel good all the time.* We live in an age that doesn't accept suffering and pain as an inevitable part of life. Some people, when feeling edgy or tense, respond by taking a tranquilizer or having a drink. When pain, physical or otherwise, invades our consciousness, we want pills or something else to solve the problem.

We also live in an age that wants instant gratification. Boredom is thought of as our worst enemy. We always need something that excites us. We need to have the TV on when we are home and the radio on when we are in the car. Silence and solitude scare us to death, even though we desperately need them to take time to reflect on our lives. We resent waiting. We hate waiting rooms and grow restless if things don't come as quickly as we like. Out of this pursuit for immediate gratification we want fast food, fast computers, and a fast lifestyle. We fail to see the self-destructiveness of our driven lives.

Part of the erroneous thinking in all of this is the false assumption that things in this world will satisfy us. They may give us temporary happiness and satisfaction, but they do not give us lasting joy. Things of this world break, wear out, and get stolen. We need to find our joy in less transient things.

Idolatrous Thought #2: *I need to have everyone like me.* Our psyches are filled with insecurities that come from our families of origin, past relationships, and self-doubts. Whenever someone doesn't like us, we become instantly afraid that our insecurities may be justified. We may be constantly on guard and wearing masks, afraid that people will find out the truth about who we are and reject us.

We may believe that keeping everyone happy is the ideal. We need to keep the peace whatever the cost. As a result, we refuse to make unpopular stands for higher truth. We may run away from conflict and confrontation when we should work through it.

We need to remember that Jesus did not keep everyone happy. He was willing to live with the reality that not everyone liked him, and he died on a cross. Are we willing to give up our need to have everyone like us? Few of us are ready to risk emotional or social crucifixion by taking an unpopular stand.

Some of us want to be with the "beautiful people." Leading citizens, solid families, and career successes are the highest hope of our social associations. We tend to avoid the drunks, the ex-cons, the poor, and the people with low social skills. Our churches are sadly homogeneous and often fail to include the down-and-out. These kind of friends were all right for Jesus but perhaps not for us.

Idolatrous Thought #3: *I need to be right all the time.* Like "Fonzie" on the old TV sitcom *Happy Days,* we're afraid to admit we might be wrong. To admit we are wrong about something is an affront to our pride and an attack on our ego. We ignore biblical injunctions to humble ourselves and follow the teachings and example of Jesus.

With this particular idolatrous thought, we often believe we are worshiping God when we are simply worshiping our ideas about God. We tend to "fit God into a box" that best suits us. We embrace ideas about God that serve us and lift up our concerns. We conveniently avoid the demands of our faith that might challenge our self-justification. Who really wants to hear about how hard it is for the rich to enter the kingdom of God (Matthew 19:24, Mark 10:25, Luke 18:25)? Who really wants to explore the implications that our works and effort count for nothing when only grace matters (Ephesians 2:8)? Can we accept that our works are nothing but evidence of the grace that dwells in us?

What we need is a large dose of humility. True humility is not putting ourselves down–it is putting ourselves in perspective. We just may be wrong about many things. And we desperately need Christian brothers and sisters to teach and correct us. It is tragic when we are so opinionated that we are unteachable.

When we reach God's kingdom, we may be surprised to learn how often we were wrong. Perhaps in heaven we will have to say things like these: "Joe, you were right about that social issue, and I was wrong. I wish I had listened to you." Or, "Mary, you really did understand God's will in that situation and I didn't. I wish I had prayed more and understood your perspective instead of being so stubborn." The good news is that we don't have to wait until heaven to begin this process. We can begin now. By God's grace, we can set aside our strong opinions and be open to what God and others seek to teach us. The truth can set us free, if we hear it.

Idolatrous Thought #4: *I need to be in control.* There is chaos in our world around us and often chaos within us. Sometimes our thoughts, feelings, impulses, and habits seem out of control. This is a tough reality to face, so denial can rear its ugly head. As a result of not being able to control ourselves, we may try to control other people, places and situations. We falsely believe that we can stop the inner turmoil by controlling everyone and everything around us.

But living to control others is often judgmental and degrading. We may think we have the answers and they don't. So we try to impose our will, our answers, and our beliefs on them. Nothing is more dangerous or more "unbiblical" than evangelism that proceeds out of this assumption. Jesus wants followers who live in his freedom, not sheep who live under the control of self-appointed authority figures.

It is time we gave up our need to control and let God be in charge. We need to stop trying to control ourselves by our own power and let God guide us. We need to stop trying to fix and manipulate our churches and church leaders and let Christ be the head of the body. We need to stop trying to dominate our families and our friends and live in mutually respectful relationships where we learn from one another.

All of these idolatrous thoughts stem from the same source. They begin with the word "I." Ego and self are the source of our sins and character defects. Self must be "crucified" before we can overcome them.

Letting God Set Us Free

When we face the truth about this self-centered sin, we know how much we need to be set free. We know God can free us and we cannot free ourselves. But how do we make it happen?

First, we become willing to let God remove all our defects of character. We need to let go of those things we cling to that enslave us. We need to recognize the self-destructiveness in our addictive behaviors. We need to give up any illusion that we have the willpower to conquer these things. We need to believe that God and God alone can take away our defects of character.

Second, we humbly ask him to remove our shortcomings. Humility is an absolute necessity in the process. We need to let go of any arrogance or delusions of importance. We need to stop focusing on our inability and focus on God's ability. We need to see his strength instead of our weakness.

Third, we ask him to take our imperfections away one at a time. Many would say that this approach seems overly simplistic and naive. They believe it fails to comprehend the complexities of human behavior and relationships. Understanding these complexities can help us understand the problem. But simply understanding things does not change them. No matter how much other people may help, healing ultimately comes from God.

God may help us through the support and encouragement of other people. Sam felt a call from God to help another in his struggle to rise above the surface of his dependency on alcohol. He sponsored this newcomer through the twelve-step program. Although this person wanted to stay sober badly, the overwhelming desire to drink haunted him almost daily. He asked Sam how he could get rid of the desire. Sam was tempted to share his own experiences with drinking and other life problems, but decided on a simple route: Sam told him to ask God every morning in his prayers to take it away. It worked. While Sam's personal sharing could have been helpful in some circumstances, this person needed to rely on God.

71

Let us also understand that when we ask God to change us, we let go of the particulars. We do not control when or how God will remove our shortcomings. Some may disappear instantly. Others may diminish gradually. Some may take years to conquer. But these character defects that seem to never go away have something important to teach us. They keep us humble and they constantly remind us of our dependency on God.

Like other needs discussed in this book, freedom is not an instant and once-and-for-all event. The road to freedom is an ongoing journey. Often we take three steps forward, then two steps back. The issue is not that we are perfect, but that we are making progress. It doesn't matter how far we need to go. It only matters that we're filled with gratitude for how far God has brought us. After all, *For freedom Christ has set us free* (Galatians 5:1a).

Chapter Seven
The Need to Heal Broken Relationships

*So when you are offering your gift at the altar,
if you remember that your brother or sister has
something against you, leave your gift there before
the altar and go; first be reconciled to your brother
or sister, and then come and offer your gift.*
Matthew 5:23-24

Donald had been sober for over 20 years. He was respected for his spiritual wisdom in the program of Alcoholics Anonymous, and he claimed Jesus Christ as his Higher Power. He was active in a local congregation and many admired his unwavering faith in spite of the many tragic experiences he had gone through.

Donald had fulfilled every step to the best of his ability. He took a yearly fourth step moral inventory of himself to make sure he maintained his spiritual fitness. There was one step that he had not completely finished. Step 9: "Made direct amends to (all persons we had harmed), except when to do so would injure them or others."

There was the unresolved matter of Vera, his first wife. They had met on a blind date when she was a devout member of a Wesleyan Church. In spite of the fact that Donald showed up drunk for their first date, they fell in love and were married in 1960. They had one son who walked with a limp because of a car accident that Donald caused while driving under the influence. In spite of many incidents like this, Donald's drinking raged on, and slowly Vera began to lose her faith and stopped going to church. She became obsessed with trying to fix Donald's alcoholism, and later came to understand that he became her higher power instead of God.

Their marriage failed and they were divorced in 1965. Both went on with their lives. Donald was married more two times:

one was a long, tumultuous relationship and the other was a short disastrous marriage. Vera also remarried and stayed with that person until a divorce in 1995.

Both Donald and Vera entered into their sixties as confirmed single people. He told his sponsor over and over that he was a self-centered, independent person and not fit to be in any relationship. She became content in the single life with her friends and her activities. She had long ago built a wall against Donald and knew he would never be part of her life again. But God had other plans. Because of his deep Christian commitment, Donald felt guilty that he had driven Vera away from her faith and the church. He knew he had to make amends to her somehow. Finally he prayed: "God, I'll do anything to get Vera back to her faith and back to church."

Donald found himself calling her even though they had not had a deep conversation in years. He found himself asking her to lunch. In spite of her walls of defense against him, Vera accepted the invitation. At this point, Donald's only intention was to make amends and encourage her to be involved again in the church. For her part, Vera had conceded that they might possibly become friends. But that was it–absolutely nothing more.

Then he showed up for the date with flowers in his hand. Vera sensed the unmistakable presence of God with him–it wasn't the same old drunken Donald. He was a kinder, sensitive, more spiritual man. She responded with a warmth she had not thought possible.

Donald was scared to death. He ran to his sponsor and poured out all his fears. Donald's sponsor told him that he never believed that Donald was too self-centered and independent for a relationship. Donald confessed he had never stopped loving Vera even though they had been apart over 30 years. His sponsor told him to move ahead in the relationship slowly and cautiously. The next Sunday, Vera went to church with Donald. That day, she recommitted her life to Jesus Christ. The relationship that they thought was dead experienced a miraculous resurrection. Within three months, they were at the altar reciting their vows and recommitting themselves to each other in Christian marriage.

The Rocky Road to Healing

Most of us have broken relationships in our history. Perhaps we were hurt by someone we used to date. Perhaps we let an important friendship drift apart. Perhaps we feel so estranged from our children or parents that we are ready to disown them. Perhaps we have so many bad feelings about some work relationships that we consciously avoid those people. Perhaps we have an ongoing personality conflict with a member of our church. Perhaps we are overwhelmed by the reality of betrayal in our marriage. Or perhaps we deal with estrangement similar to that experienced by Adam and Claire:

Adam and Claire were brother and sister. They had been reasonably close as they grew up together. Claire was three years older and had always felt a responsibility for her "little brother," even when he came to be six inches taller and sixty pounds heavier. As adults, they had returned home with their families at Easter, Thanksgiving, and Christmas. They had both visited their mother repeatedly during the struggle with cancer which eventually took her life.

Shortly after their mother's death, their father died of a heart attack with no warning at all. His will had been made twenty years ago, with no knowledge of how many grandchildren there would be. He made Claire the executor of the estate, left no money directly to Adam or Claire but rather specified equal shares to all living grandchildren, and authorized Claire to make any adjustments in the terms of the will that seemed necessary.

The problem was that Claire had four children, and Adam's one child had died in a tragic accident six months before Adam and Claire's mother died. Thus all of the estate went to Claire's children with nothing to Adam or his family. To make matters more complicated, Claire and her husband had a very high income; and Adam and his wife were barely getting by. Claire, thinking that she was being fair by going beyond the requirements of the will, gave $25,000 to Adam. The total estate, however, had come to almost a million dollars; and $25,000 seemed like very little to Adam. They had a horrible fight when Claire gave him the check, and he refused to sign a statement that he would make no other claims on the estate. Instead he hired an attorney and went to court in an effort to receive a larger amount of the estate, convinced that his father never

75

intended for him to receive so little. Claire was furious and vowed to fight Adam in court, but her attorney urged her to make a settlement and avoid creating an even deeper rift in the family. She reluctantly gave Adam $250,000 in exchange for an agreement that there would be no other claims against the estate. She felt as though Adam had stolen the money from her children.

Ten years later, Claire had cancer herself and began looking back on her life. There were no hurts that felt as deep as the alienation from her brother, whom she had loved so dearly growing up. She wondered why her father had made out the will in such a way and then recognized that he had done it before she or Adam had children. He could not have anticipated the disparity it would create. He probably thought little about the will, given the grief following the death of a grandchild and the death of his wife. She thought about the difficulty of Adam's life, about the loss of his child, and about the financial struggles he had experienced. The $250,000 no longer seemed like such a loss. She wished her father had simply divided the estate equally between herself and Adam. And then she realized that her father had given her the latitude as executor to make any changes that were needed. She had lost her brother over money, when she and her husband already had everything they needed. She realized that her anger had alienated her from God as well as from Adam.

She wrote a letter of apology to Adam in which she said that she wanted to give him another $250,000 and that she prayed they could become close again. Adam, however, still angry over what had happened, threw her letter away and did not answer it. After three weeks went by, Claire called Adam's home and ended up talking to his wife, who informed her that Adam did not want money from her and did not want anything to do with her. Adam would come to feel differently; but unfortunately that feeling would come at the time of Claire's funeral.

Many of us are inclined to leave broken relationships in the past and would prefer to forget about them. "Time heals all wounds," we explain. We believe that broken relationships in the past don't affect how we conduct our present relationships. But if this is true, why do we persist in the same unhealthy behavior in relationships? The passage of time brought no automatic healing for Claire and Adam; and following Claire's death, there was no way for the relationship to be healed. Attempts at reconciliation can only go as far as the other person is willing to be reconciled.

The Path to Reconciliation

Jesus suggested an alternative course of action in his teachings on peacemaking. Too many assume that peacemaking involves being passive. We are supposed to let people abuse us and then walk away while we feel torn apart inside. Peacemaking is not a passive endeavor, but a very active one. And Jesus told us what that action should be: to *go and be reconciled with your brother or sister. . .*

But Jesus told us something even more frightening: we cannot correctly worship God until we have been reconciled with others. He told us to leave our gift at the altar to go and be reconciled. He told us our gifts to God are meaningless unless we live at peace with others. We cannot use our gift to buy absolution. Until we have done all we can to be reconciled, our worship is empty.

Furthermore, Jesus told us to go directly to the person we have a conflict with. He did not tell us to judge them or gossip about them or ignore them. He told us to go directly to them. Nothing else can deal with the situation. Most problems in families, churches, and other groups could be avoided if we went directly to the other person instead of behind their backs.

First John clearly tells us that our relationship with God and our relationship with others are interdependent and serve as mirror images of each other: *Those who say, 'I love God," and hate their brothers or sisters, are liars; for those who do not love a brother or sister whom they have seen, cannot love God whom they have not seen.* As well as strongly upholding the ideal of peacemaking in relationships, the Bible understands that not all relationships can be healed. Many times the other person is unresponsive to our overtures and stubborn in his or her hostility. At this point, we cannot take responsibility for the failure of this attempt at reconciliation. Paul places a helpful condition on interpersonal peacemaking: *If it is possible, so far as it depends on you, live peaceably with all.* This "if" tells us that we are only responsible for cleaning up our side of the street.

There are at least four practical steps we can take in healing broken relationships. They are: 1) avoid the blame game, 2) make amends to those we have harmed, 3) forgive those who have harmed us, and 4) learn healthier ways to relate to others. Let us explore each of these steps.

Step One: Avoid the Blame Game. We think blaming puts one person in an advantaged position. We cultivate unhealthy fantasies of the other person coming to us on their knees, saying all the blame belonged to them, and begging for forgiveness. But seldom are broken relationships the fault of just one side of the relationship. Even if we only hold ten percent of the responsibility for the brokenness, we need to deal with that ten percent.

There are two ways that blame can be harmful. First, we can blame others, avoiding responsibility for our part in creating brokenness. We may feel like we are right, but the relationship is still broken.

Second, we can blame ourselves, thinking that any wrongful encounter is a product of only our behavior. Too many people blame themselves when something is wrong in any relationship. We spend hours reliving interactions we had with others trying to figure out what we did wrong. We jump to the conclusion that it is always our fault if someone is unhappy.

Blame very seldom solves problems. Unhealthy families or groups are known for arguing for hours or even days, debating who was really at fault. They spend so much time and energy focusing on fault that they fail to deal with the real problem. Often the blame habitually falls on one person, making him or her the "scapegoat." Families and other groups would be better served by working together on what could be done to rectify the problem. Fixing blame fixes nothing.

Step 2: Make amends. Making amends is about acknowledging how we contributed to the broken relationship. Realizing one's own faults and accepting healthy responsibility for them is good practice for resolving issues with others.

Though it is painful, we should identify the broken relationships in our lives and reflect on the role that we have played in that brokenness. We need to carefully examine the broken relationships where we feel "faultless" and be honest about our part in the brokenness. This examination usually involves extensive prayer–asking God to give us the willingness to make amends to each person on the list.

We should make amends directly to such people whenever possible, as long it does not harm the other person. We cannot accomplish this without God's strength. By making direct amends, we are often putting ourselves in a vulnerable position in front of someone we consider "unsafe." We are opening ourselves up to more criticism, rejection, and the denial of forgiveness. These fears are very real. The other person may be harsh with us. Perhaps all we may ever get is "thank you."

But we are making amends for our own sake as much as or even more than for the other person. No longer will we have haunting thoughts and feelings that we have left something undone. We are not making amends so everyone will like us. We are making amends so we can like ourselves. If the other person refuses to forgive us, it is not our fault. We are responsible for changing ourselves, not changing them. That is a project best left up to them and God.

We need to remember what Paul wrote: *If it is possible, as far as it depends on you. . .* If we have truly been forgiven by God and have forgiven ourselves, the other person's forgiveness becomes secondary in importance. Also, we are doing much more than cleaning up the past by making amends. We are freeing ourselves in the present and opening up new possibilities for our future. We no longer need to carry baggage from past broken relationships into future relationships.

There is one caution in making amends to others. We should not do so if our words will cause further hurt or pain. For example, it is not prudent for a man to tell his friend he has been having an affair with that person's wife. There is a proper time and a proper place for making amends. If the time is right, God will provide the opportunity. We must never make amends without first praying about it.

Consider an example. John hesitated making amends for his infidelities until he felt it was absolutely the right time and place. In his own addictive behavior, he badly hurt many women. He avoided making amends to two of them because they were married, and their husbands may not have taken kindly to another man writing to their wives. When one woman ended her marriage in divorce, John then wrote a letter of amends to her. When the other woman lost her husband to cancer and some time had passed for her to grieve, he then wrote an amends letter to her. We are making amends on God's timing, not ours.

Sometimes the person we have harmed is dead or unable to be found. Nevertheless, we can still do our part to make amends. Many people have visited the grave site of someone they have harmed and confessed their wrongdoing to a tombstone. Most of the people who have done this feel like the other person "heard" their confession even though they were no longer alive. Other people have written letters to "lost" people. While the actual amends have not been made, there is a great feeling of relief on the part of the person who makes the effort.

Step 3: Forgive Others. Carrying resentments or grudges does far more damage to us than we can imagine. Resentment does little to harm the person we resent, but much to harm us while we are carrying the resentment. Forgiveness and letting go are the only healthy ways out. As Christ has forgiven us, so must we forgive others.

True forgiveness does not come fast or easy. It is not a denial of our pain. It is slowly and prayerfully letting go of holding the other person responsible for it. Forgiveness is a choice we make, one in which we often have to move through deep feelings. While forgiveness confirms that our hurt is real, it allows us to feel free–free from guilt, hurt, or the need to condemn ourselves and others.

We need to forgive those who have offended us. We need to look at and deal with our pain and resentments. We need to do this for our own healing. It is a wonderful thing if the relationship is healed. More importantly, we must be healed if we are going to become all God created us to be.

One of the best techniques for forgiveness is sometimes called the "resentment prayer." This means praying for the health, prosperity, and well-being of every person we resent. We will not pray that our agenda be done in their lives, but that God's agenda be done. We need to use this prayer every day for two weeks. If we miss a day, we need to start over again. At first, we feel like phonies praying for people we resent. But eventually, our prayers will change our hearts and we will find ourselves having kinder spirits toward those who have hurt us. There is not a simple formula for this prayer, but it is important to pray for these people by name and to be as specific as possible in asking God to bless their lives. In the Sermon on the Mount, Jesus told us: ". . . love your enemies and pray for those who persecute you" (Matthew 5:44). The Apostle Paul concurred: "Bless those who persecute you; bless and do not curse them" (Romans 12:14).

Step 4: Learn Healthier Ways to Relate to Others. All the healing of past brokenness will do us little good if we continue to make the same mistakes in our present relationships. We need to let go of defects in how we relate and find healthier ways. If we fail to do this, we will go through the same painful process again and again.

Professional counseling may be very helpful if we have severe problems in relating to others. However, short of professional counseling, there are some concrete actions we can take. We can begin this process by listing all of our defects that harm our relationships, such as gossip, blaming, and taking criticism too personally. It is helpful to work on this list of problem relationship behaviors for several days so we can have an extensive and thorough list. On the same page, opposite each problem behavior, we need to write more positive and healthy relationship behaviors. For example, instead of gossiping, we can write that we will learn to go directly to people we have trouble with and talk things out honestly.

Read the list of problems and the list of alternative behaviors each day for at least two weeks and submit them to God in prayer. If possible, share these lists with a sponsor or mentor and talk about ways to change our behavior. We should ask a sponsor, mentor, or support group to hold us accountable, asking for their prayers and honest feedback. Healthier relationship behavior will happen, but not overnight. It is an ongoing, lifelong process.

When we do the four steps involved in healing broken relationships, some amazing things will happen to us. The *Big Book of Alcoholics Anonymous* describes them as "Promises." They truly are remarkable promises for a better future:

If we are painstaking about this phase of our development, we will be amazed before we are halfway through. We are going to know a new freedom and a new happiness. We will not regret the past nor wish to shut the door on it. We will comprehend the word serenity and we will know peace. No matter how far down the scale we have gone, we will see how our experience can benefit others. That feelings of uselessness and self-pity will disappear. We will lose interest in selfish things and gain interest in others. Self-seeking will slip away. Our whole attitude and outlook upon life will change. Fear of people and of economic insecurity will leave us. We will intuitively know how to handle situations which used to baffle us. We will suddenly realize that God is doing for us what we could not do for ourselves.

Are these extravagant promises? We think not. They are being fulfilled among us–sometimes quickly, sometimes slowly. They will materialize if we work for them. [pp. 83-84]

True reconciliation can be achieved only when we have God's help. Keeping in mind the people we have hurt, those who have brought us pain, and the healing by God through prayer will lift our spirits. We will be reminded of life's fragility. Our love for friends and family can always be renewed with a willingness on our part and God's sacred gifts of forgiveness and mercy. Joan Hershey describes it beautifully in her memoir *Forever in Love*: "Life is so very, very precious and nothing should keep us from spending time with our loved ones while we have them with us" (p. 79).

The bottom line paradox of healing broken relationships is this: If we set out to heal broken relationships with others, we will ultimately heal ourselves.

Chapter Eight
The Need for Intimacy with God

> You are my friends if you do what I
> command you.   John 15:14

In order to show an example of God's love and mercy to those who have addictions, Sam describes some painful experiences from his own life:

As a young boy I was a good "Christian" young person. I was in church every Sunday. My jacket lapel boasted a string of perfect attendance pins. Every week in Sunday School, I asked us to sing "The Old Rugged Cross." When they had open prayer time, I always volunteered a prayer for those not in attendance. Sunday School teachers loved to have me in their class because of my exemplary Christian behavior.

When I was 10 years old, a deacon named Paul Witzman took our Sunday School class on a tour of the sanctuary. When we came to the baptistry, he said, "This is where you are baptized when you accept Christ as your Savior." Something about his words cut me to the heart. I wanted Jesus as my Savior and I wanted him right now! After going through a membership class, I went through the waters of baptism.

At age 12, a pastor preached a sermon that also touched my heart. He talked about how God desperately needed our help in the world. I believed I was supposed to go into full-time Christian service. I knew I could not handle being a foreign missionary, so I decided to be a pastor.

As I entered my teen years, I became more active in my faith. I read the Bible through three times (although I didn't understand most of it). I was repeatedly elected president of the junior high and senior high youth groups. This seemed very strange and ironic for a teenage boy who was a loner at school and had no friends. I would often enter deep religious discussions with others in the group and occasionally tried to "witness" to an unchurched friend.

When I left for college, I totally rebelled. I immediately stopped attending church, even though I attended a church-related college. Profanity that I once abhorred filled my mouth.. My hair grew longer and I protested against the church because it refused to speak out on current issues.

My friends in college were into drugs, so I participated by smoking hashish, marijuana, opium, and using an hallucinogenic. At the end of my freshman year of college, I had a bad experience with drugs, so I decided to quit. I took, what seemed to me, the next logical step and began drinking heavily. When I wasn't drunk or high, I looked for solace in extremely unhealthy dating relationships. Toward the end of my college years, I became heavily interested in Yoga and Zen meditation, even minoring in Oriental philosophy.

It's hard not to notice the contrast between the beginning of my faith story and my early adult life. I was considered a fine "Christian" young man destined to be a pastor. But something was missing in my hunger for intimacy with God. Even though I was tremendously interested in things of God and the church, there was a deep, gnawing emptiness inside me. I turned my back on God and the church, determined to do what I wanted. Unfortunately, most of the things I wanted to do were terribly self-destructive. I did not reenter areas of faith, spirituality, and church involvement until I was 27 and began working a 12-step program of recovery. My spiritual program of recovery showed me approaches to intimacy with God that I failed to learn in my Christian upbringing.

I have experientially learned five faith realities that serve to fill the emptiness in my soul: 1) I need God and His abundant grace in all areas of my life; 2) my life can only be lived in daily dependence on God for all things; 3) all my relationships, especially with God, require total honesty; 4) God isn't determined to punish me, but determined to love me; and 5) God, not self, is the center of all things. Ironically, all of these things are strong biblical principles that I learned in recovery rather than the church.

Like many recovering alcoholics and addicts, I now thank God for my addictions. I do not thank Him for the misery I caused myself and others. I thank Him because, without my addictions, I *would not have discovered the intimacy. I continue to attend meetings and work the steps not so much to stay clean and sober, as to grow in my intimacy with God.*

I must caution you that I have not "arrived," and have far to go in my Christian journey. There are times when I doubt the sincerity of my faith, but I am heading in the right direction. I have learned that it really doesn't matter whether we are close to God or far away. What matters is the direction our lives are going, either toward him or away from him.

Our Need for Spiritual Intimacy

Sam suspects that many who are reading this have experienced some of the same things he has. Outwardly, we have strong religious lives, but inwardly we feel spiritually empty. Our souls yearn to be in touch with who God *is* in a very personal and direct way. When a person encounters God even in the simplest way, it can be a life-transforming experience–enabling one to look at the world in a whole different light.

Intimacy with God is the deepest hunger of the human heart. St. Augustine wrote: *Our hearts are restless until they find rest in Thee.* It's hard to ignore our need for spiritual intimacy. It's what gives our lives integrity and meaning.

The need for intimacy with God is why the person of Jesus Christ means so much to us. He destroys all the barriers and makes intimacy with God possible. He boldly proclaims that we can be his friends. We are more than servants, more than disciples, and more than followers. We are his friends. Our only qualification for this special role is to seek to do God's will in our lives on a daily basis.

The primary purpose of the church is to help people experience God and let God begin to transform their lives. When we truly let God transform our lives, we will begin to do many things differently and will view service and mission in an entirely different way than before. But we must be clear about what is really important. Fifty years ago, C.S. Lewis warned in his classic book *Mere Christianity* that it is easy for us to get confused:

> *It is so easy to get muddled about this. It is easy to*
> *think that the Church has a lot of different objects–*
> *education, building, missions, holding services. . . .*
> *[T]he church exists for nothing else but to draw*
> *[people] into Christ, to make them little Christs.*
> *If they are not doing that, all the cathedrals, clergy,*
> *missions, sermons, even the Bible itself, are simply*
> *a waste of time. God became Man for no other*
> *purpose. It is even doubtful, you know, whether*
> *the whole universe was created for any other*
> *purpose.*

But as much as we desire intimacy with God and the transformation of our lives, there is a part of ourselves that resists it. At times, it is easier to have a formal, businesslike relationship with God. We are afraid of intimacy because it requires so much work and effort. According to 1 John 4:12, intimacy with God is difficult because it requires us to first be intimate with each other.

The biblical image of God as our heavenly "Father" can also create barriers. Many of us rejoice in this image and gladly call God "Abba–Daddy." But those who have suffered at the hands of an earthly father are not as comfortable with the concept of God as "Father." We are reminded that people tend to put the face of their own father or mother on the face of God. Our image of a heavenly parent is often the image of our earthly family.

Two important things need to be said to those who struggle with the concept of God as their heavenly Father because of the actions of their earthly fathers. First, there are several biblical images that convey a more motherly image of God (for example: Isaiah 49:15, Luke 13:34). People who have suffered abuse from a father or mother may benefit from focusing more on the other parental image for God.

Second, the previous chapters have dealt with recovery in many areas of our lives. We can also recover from our parental memories. The steps we have outlined in this book help us to overcome feelings and attitudes we associate with the words "father" or "mother." We need to be reminded that God is totally unlike an abusive or neglectful parent–God is a healthy and loving heavenly Parent for all people.

The Need for Intimacy with God

Achieving Intimacy with God

With all of this in mind, let us look at ways we can work at being more intimate with God. There are many fine books, such as *Celebration of Discipline* by Richard Foster, that show us how to practice spiritual disciplines to grow closer to God. Here we would like to identify five spiritual disciplines that have been repeatedly recognized as essential to successful recovery and spirituality.

The first discipline is *prayer*. We must pray daily. We cannot build a friendship with someone we talk with infrequently. We need regular contact to grow closer. The same holds true for our relationship with God.

To be effective, prayer should express our total dependency on God in all things. We must humbly realize that we can do nothing without His help. We must be honest. Religious platitudes and biblical slogans do not constitute a meaningful prayer life. However, prayers from our heart that express our deepest needs create intimacy with God. Our search for intimacy stems from our own vulnerability. Prayer must also continually express a deep desire to do God's will in our daily lives.

Recited prayers are also helpful. The Serenity Prayer and the Lord's Prayer are almost always used at 12-step meetings. Members often recite them over and over to themselves when they are in a difficult situation. With repetition, the meaning of the prayer deepens. The Lord's Prayer can be found in Matthew 6:9-13. The words to the Serenity Prayer are credited to Reinhold Niebuhr:

God, grant me the serenity
to accept the things I cannot change,
the courage to change the things I can,
and the wisdom to know the difference.
Living one day at a time,
enjoying one moment at a time;
accepting hardship as a pathway to peace;
taking, as Jesus did,
this sinful world as it is,
not as I would have it;
trusting that you will make all things right
if I surrender to your will;

87

so that I may be reasonably happy in this life
and supremely happy with you forever in the next.
Amen.

The second spiritual discipline required for spiritual recovery is *meditation.* We must not only talk with God; we must listen to him. Too often we are so busy listening to other voices in our heads that we fail to hear the voice of God. We hear that we are never good enough. We hear all the demands we have for our day. We hear the voices of those who doubt us, criticize us, and put us down. These voices can be loud like a strong wind, or an earthquake, or a raging fire. But like the prophet Elijah, we need to listen to the voice of God in the silence (I Kings 19:11-13). In our own daily prayer time, we can leave several minutes to listen to God. We can wait for his response and end up in deep spiritual communion. God can also speak with us through the Bible, another reading, or a trusted friend.

The third spiritual discipline we must practice is *study.* We agree with most writers on the discipline of study who say that the Bible is the most important book we can use. People who are in recovery or who are interested in better understanding those in recovery have found these versions very helpful: *The NIV Recovery Bible* and *The Life Recovery Bible (TLB).* Both of these wonderful texts include devotional readings on such issues as resentment, forgiveness, and accountability. They carefully take the reader through the 12 steps of recovery from a biblical perspective.

There is also a wealth of other literature we can study. In any Christian bookstore, we can find recovery books on all kinds of topics from codependency to overeating. While many secular recovery books are not overtly Christian, they still convey many Christian values. Melody Beattie, John Bradshaw, Leo Buscaglia, and Pia Mellody are especially helpful authors for persons in recovery or wanting to better understand recovery. We can also gain a great deal from reading books about the spiritual life which are not directly related to the topic of recovery. The books, for example, of C.S. Lewis, Thomas Merton, Henri Nouwen, and Richard Foster can help us in our efforts to grow closer to God.

The fourth necessary discipline is having a *spiritual director, mentor, or sponsor* with whom we can meet regularly. Denial and rationalization are such an integral part of our make-up that we need someone who cares enough to tell us the truth. Sam's sponsor recently confronted him about his growing cynicism, defensiveness, and negativism in conversations. Since his confrontation, things have been heading a more positive direction. Here are some guidelines for choosing a spiritual director, mentor, or sponsor:

- Find someone with whom you can be comfortable meeting on a regular basis. This might be telephone contact once a week or a meeting in a restaurant twice a month.
- Choose someone who has a spirituality you can respect.
- Find someone who is safe and keeps confidences.
- Find someone who will be honest with you and not just tell you what you want to hear.

Explain to that person why you would like a mentoring relationship and what would be involved. If he or she claims to be too inexperienced or lacking in knowledge, the humility itself may stand as a qualification! Set up a schedule for regular telephone and face-to-face contacts. Finally, hold each other accountable for keeping these scheduled appointments. Pray together at every meeting.

The fifth and final discipline is accountability to a *spiritually-based support group*. Once we have achieved intimacy with God, it is much easier to be intimate with others. Sunday School classes and continuing Bible studies sometimes lack the intimacy and depth that is required. Those classes and studies, however, can sometimes be transformed if those who are part of the groups want to do so. The addition of a "joys and concerns" time to group meetings, a covenant to keep confidential what is shared in these groups, and a commitment to pray for one another can transform the life of these groups.

Sometimes it is best to form a group of people who are struggling with the same issue, whether it be divorce, addiction, overeating, deepening the spiritual life, or something else. Share your experience, strength, and hope with each other. Listen and learn as they share their struggles with the same issues. Above all, agree to keep all discussions confidential.

Reaching the Pinnacle. . .

Dealing with painful personal issues and broken relationships can be hard work. But as you reach greater intimacy with God, your life is transformed. We are no longer just healing the past, but growing toward the future. We begin to discover God, not just in church, but in daily life. A friend of Sam's named Ed, who has dealt with recovery issues, shared this poem:

> *I sought to hear the voice of God*
> *And climbed the topmost steeple*
> *But God declared , "Go down again,*
> *I dwell among the people."*

Chapter Nine
The Need for Spiritual Power

> But (God) said to me, 'My grace is
> sufficient for you, for my power is made
> perfect in weakness.
>   2 Corinthians 12:8, NIV

Until she entered recovery and deeper spirituality, Elizabeth almost always felt powerless. She was raised the oldest child of a German farm family, attended a very strict church, and was never encouraged to talk about emotions or needs. The words used to describe emotions were practically a foreign language to her. Elizabeth also had a younger brother named George. George was sickly from birth and had his first major seizure when he was five months old. This episode began a history of repeated crises with many trips to the emergency room. Elizabeth's mother lived in continuing fear that George would have a seizure and die.

Instead of surrendering her fears and worries to God, Elizabeth's mother acted as if the family must be in constant vigil to keep George from dying. If George died, they had failed. Everything done around the home was designed to protect George from a possibly fatal seizure.

Naturally, this impacted Elizabeth. The family message was very clear: protect George no matter what the cost to yourself or the family. Trust no one else to take care of us, and sometimes, do not even trust God. Elizabeth received the message that her feelings and needs were irrelevant and only George mattered. She secretly harbored deep resentments toward her sickly brother, but hid behind a mask of passivity and social withdrawal.

Implicit in all of this was a clear message to Elizabeth about relating to people and the world: The world is a terrible place and will destroy you if you are not constantly vigilant. Elizabeth learned that is was important to:

- Always play life by the rules.
- Always be a "people pleaser" by keeping everyone around her happy.
- Change the world where possible.
- Recognize that she was too weak to handle this terrible world.

All of these guidelines except the third put Elizabeth in a powerless position. Without realizing it, she focused for a time on the third and went to college and graduate school to become a social worker. She tried to make an impact, but often felt powerless in facing the overwhelming problems of this "terrible world." In both her job and personal life, she responded to her own anger by crying and feeling helpless.

During graduate school, she met regularly with some Christian students. With their help, she grew out of a strict, businesslike faith into a more dynamic and intimate relationship with God. She developed a closer relationship with Christ and learned to trust others and receive their help in growing in the faith.

Still, for many years, Elizabeth continued to play a helpless, powerless role. She saw herself as a perpetual victim in life and withdrew as much as she could. She remained active in church, hanging on to her newfound spirituality as her only consolation. When she did enter relationships, Elizabeth found herself becoming hopelessly codependent and victimized.

After marrying a kind man who shared her faith, Elizabeth's problems became more evident. At the urging of her husband, she began attending meetings of Codependents Anonymous and seeing a professional counselor. Counseling helped her face and confront the ghosts of her past. She also learned to set boundaries so that the things people did around her and to her would not have a devastating effect on her.

In her 12-step recovery, she discovered her own worth by understanding how much God loved her. She began to get in touch with her needs and emotions and even learned the language of feelings. Slowly, she became more and more assertive when people tried to take advantage of her. She still cried when angry, but stood her ground with all confrontations.

Elizabeth is now a successful professional and is growing closer to her husband all the time. She often teaches Sunday School classes for new Christians, offering them a deeper spirituality than she had growing up. She lives life with hope and a sense of adventure, trusting that God will take care of her through all difficulties.

Spiritual Powerlessness

Chapter Eight discussed *The Need for Intimacy with God.* We all need greater intimacy to God and a willingness to turn our lives more fully over to God. When we truly open our hearts and minds to God, we begin to experience transformation–sometimes in ways we never anticipated.

C.S. Lewis suggested in his writings that turning one's life over to God is a little like going to a very good dentist because of a toothache. One goes to the dentist to get relief from the immediate pain, and that relief is generally provided. A good dentist, however, will examine the rest of one's mouth and will be alert for other areas which are in need of improvement. There may be teeth which are not yet hurting which show the early signs of disease and are in need of repair. There may be tartar build-up or gum disease of which one was not aware. The good dentist, if permitted to do so, will continue until one's overall oral health has been significantly improved.

God, in fact, seeks to make us perfect. That's obviously not a goal which will be fully achieved in this lifetime, but it is the direction in which God seeks to help us move–to the extent that we are willing to do so. Lewis describes the process in this way in *Mere Christianity:*

> *The command* Be ye perfect *is not idealistic gas.
> Nor is it a command to do the impossible. He is
> going to make us into creatures that can obey that
> command. . . . If we let Him–for we can prevent Him,
> if we choose–He will make the feeblest and filthiest
> of us into a god or goddess, a dazzling, radiant,
> immortal creature, pulsating all through with such*

> *energy and joy and wisdom and love as we cannot*
> *now imagine, a bright stainless mirror which reflects*
> *back to God perfectly (though, of course, on a smaller*
> *scale) His own boundless power and delight and*
> *goodness.* [Macmillan, 1943, 1945, 1952 p. 176]

Many people who are caught up in addictions or in other major problems feel that they are powerless to change, unable to make their lives different. People who live with those who struggle with such problems can also feel an overwhelming sense of powerlessness. They especially feel powerless when those they help have already taken control of their lives and they find themselves unable to do so.

There are people who have no apparent addictions who nevertheless feel powerless in many aspects of their lives. Consider, for example:

- Brad is working on his doctorate at a large
  university and receives a tuition waiver and spending
  money by working as a research assistant to a
  professor. As a part of that work, Brad made a
  discovery which was a major advance in that field
  of inquiry. His professor took full credit for Brad's
  work and did not even list Brad as a second author
  on the three published papers which Brad wrote.
  Brad feels taken advantage of and powerless to do
  anything to gain credit for his contributions.

- Becky has lived as a foster child for the past
  three years. She was sexually abused in her first
  foster home. She was unable to convince the social
  worker of what had happened to her, but she was
  moved to another home. Although she wasn't abused
  in the next home, she found herself living like an
  unpaid servant, who was released to go to school
  but not for any other purpose. She did the laundry,
  prepared the meals, and kept the house clean, while
  the two natural children of the foster parents were
  able to participate in normal activities.

- Bill has always worked hard and has stayed with the
  same company for years. He knows that he lacks
  the political skills to build relationships with those

who are above him in the organization, but he feels he has always done excellent work. He finds time after time that employees who do not work as hard receive promotions which Bill believes should have been his.

• Sally is a fifteen-year-old diabetic. She has learned how to test her own blood sugar and to determine the amount of insulin she should take, but it feels to her as though the disease strangles her life. When she changed schools because her family moved, she was accused of illegal drug use because a teacher saw her with a syringe. She feels as though her friends either pity her because of the diabetes or are uncomfortable because of her need to prick her own finger four times a day and use a portable instrument to find our her sugar level. She feels like a victim of the diabetes.

All of those persons feel out of control in important aspects of their lives. All four of them are involved in a church and think of themselves as Christians, but they have not experienced the transformation which is made available by turning life over to God's care.

Anne Lamott, in *Traveling Mercies*, writes about her own struggles with addiction and the lengths to which she went to cover that addiction:

> *I took a sleeping pill with the last glass of Scotch every night, woke up late, wrote for a couple of hours, and then walked to one of four local liquor stores to buy a pint of Dewars. Back at Pat's, I would pour the whiskey back into the big bottle, raising the level back to where it had been before I started the night before. Then I'd put the empty in a brown paper bag and take off for the bike path to dispose of it.* [p. 38]

Anne Lamott's life changed through her belief in God and through her contact with caring people in the Christian community. She gained the power to take control of her own life, and she became a successful author. That same power is available to all of us.

95

The Meaning of Spiritual Power

Jesus is the center of our understanding of spiritual power. Jesus' power came from his Father: "Very truly, I tell you, the Son can do nothing on his own, but only what he sees the Father doing; for whatever the Father does, the Son does likewise" (John 5:19). As we look at this reality of spiritual power in the life and teachings of Jesus, four truths become apparent.

First, Jesus received his power through his own humiliation. Even though he was the Son of God, he allowed himself to be humiliated by becoming a common man, taking the form of a servant, and suffering a criminal's death. Paul writes: "(he) emptied himself, taking the form of a slave, being born in human likeness. And being found in human form, he humbled himself and became obedient to the point of death–even death on a cross. Therefore God also highly exalted him and gave him the name that is above every name" (Philippians 2:7-9).

Second, Jesus revealed his power throughout his earthly ministry. There was power in his teaching, "for he taught them as one having authority. . ." (Matthew 7:29). He exercised his power against anything that diminished people; and "he cured many who were sick with various diseases, and cast out many demons. . ." (Mark 1:34). Even spiritual evil could not prevail against him. "When he (Legion) saw Jesus from a distance, he ran and bowed down before him; and he shouted at the top of his voice, 'What have you to do with me, Jesus, Son of the Most High God? I adjure you by God, do not torment me'" (Mark 5:6-7). Ultimately, he exercised great spiritual power in his resurrection and opened the door to eternal life.

Third, Jesus coupled his spiritual power with compassion. His power was always used for the good of others and never for self-serving reasons. "When he went ashore, he saw a great crowd; and he had compassion for them and cured their sick" (Matthew 14:14). After this verse, Jesus further displayed his spiritual power by miraculously feeding over 5,000 people. Too many people present a sad distortion of the gospel when they misuse "spiritual power" by seeking to exercise it over others with little or no compassion. Paul warned against this when he wrote: "if I have prophetic powers, and understand all mysteries and all knowledge, and if I have all faith, so as to remove mountains, but do not have love, I am nothing" (1 Corinthians 13;2).

It is equally disastrous when we talk about Christian compassion and leave out the spiritual power that must be coupled with it. Jesus had compassion on many, and He had the power to do something about it. Spiritual power was an integral part of His life-changing ministry. This is why Jesus described in this way the healing of the woman who continually hemorrhaged: "'Someone must have touched me for I noticed that power had gone out from me'" (Luke 8:46).

We can have compassion on a child with a severe toothache, but until we exercise the power to take him to the dentist, our compassion will do no good. We can care about someone who is struggling with cancer and visit her regularly, but until we pray for her with power, we can offer support but not God's healing. We can suffer in a relationship where we are abused by an employer, a spouse, or church member, but we can still feel powerless to change it. Until we decide to free ourselves from the powerless victim role and exercise our God-given spiritual power, nothing will change.

The final and most important aspect of the spiritual power found in Jesus is this: Jesus gives this same power to his believers. He told us about the power of a group of believers praying and working together: "'Truly I tell you, whatever you bind on earth will be bound in heaven, and whatever you loose on earth will be loosed in heaven. Again, truly I tell you, if two of you agree on earth about anything you ask it will be done for you by my Father in heaven'" (Matthew 18:18-19).

At the Last Supper, Jesus made this promise: "'Very truly, I tell you, the one who believes in me will also do the works that I do and, in fact, will do greater works than these. . .'" (John 14:12). After His resurrection and before His ascension into heaven, Jesus gave His ultimate promise of the spiritual power that belongs to believers: "'But you will receive power when the Holy Spirit has come upon you; and you will be my witnesses in Jerusalem, in all Judea and Samaria, and to the ends of the earth'" (Acts 1:8).

The manner in which God works in our lives and helps us discover spiritual power can vary greatly from person to person.

Rebecca and Amy both went through painful divorces and had a great need to forgive their ex-husbands and not let the past become a barrier to the future. Both of them found significant help through deepened spiritual lives and through the same divorced persons support group in a local church. Rebecca, following a prayer circle one evening in the support group, felt the entire burden of her anger about the past lifted from her. She was able to forgive her ex-husband, to recognize her own contributions to the failed marriage, and to truly put those painful memories behind her.

Amy likewise felt significantly helped as she deepened her personal prayer life, shared her concerns with the church group, and received the supportive prayers of others, including those of Rebecca with whom she developed a deep friendship. For Amy, however, it was impossible to immediately put behind her all the hurt and resentment of the past. She recognized the validity of what Rebecca experienced and prayed for the same thing to happen in her own life, but she did not gain a sense of empowerment so quickly. She did find, as she continued to pray and to talk honestly with others, that her resentment and bitterness began to fade. As she talked to Rebecca at lunch one day three years after joining the support group, Amy realized that she had left behind virtually all of the anger and that she genuinely felt forgiving toward her ex-husband.

We need to remain aware that we are each different, and that God relates in a unique way to each one of us. It's wonderful to read the insights of people like C.S. Lewis and to hear the success stories of people like Anne Lamott, Rebecca, and Amy. We nevertheless need to recognize that our own experiences of God's power will not be identical to those of others. The experiences of another person should not become the standard by which we evaluate the validity of our own lives or our own closeness to God. God's empowerment comes to us all, but the speed and means may differ greatly from what others experience. There is a wonderful paradox in the gift of spiritual power. Such spiritual power is not given to the strong. It is given to the weak, the powerless, and the suffering. That is why God answered Paul's petition for healing: "My grace is sufficient for you, for my power is made perfect in weakness" (2 Corinthians 12:8, NIV). Our vulnerability and our humility are the keys to God releasing spiritual power into our lives.

The theme of the 12 steps of recovery could be summed up in the word "power." Three of the steps even use the word directly. Step One begins: *We admitted we were powerless over (fill in the blank), and our lives had become unmanageable.* We cannot begin to be transformed by God's power until we admit utter defeat and realize that we are powerless to change our situation.

Step Two gives us hope of a new source of power when it says: We *came to believe that a Power greater than ourselves could restore us to sanity.* We do not have the power, but thankfully, God does. And He loves us so much that, if we let Him, He can change us when we cannot change ourselves. This is a saving hope.

Step Eleven also mentions spiritual power: *praying only for knowledge of God's will for us and the power to carry that out.* If we pray for the power to do God's will, he will give it to us. What a turnaround! We started utterly powerless and defeated. Now we have the spiritual power to do anything that God wants us to do. There are no limits to what we can do for God.

Before we overdo this proclamation of spiritual power, let us look at two common abuses of it. The number one abuse of power is using it to control people, places, and situations. As mentioned in Chapter Six, the need to be in control is an idol. We are wrong when we try to manipulate, use, or push people around. God grants each person the freedom of choice to move toward him or away from him. Therefore, we must grant each other that same freedom. We must not misuse our spiritual authority to manipulate other Christians into our way of thinking.

The second abuse of spiritual power is to react completely against it with passivity. Like Elizabeth, we too often go through life feeling like victims of everything. We let people hurt us and do nothing. We are afraid we will rock the boat and people will be unhappy with us. We are afraid to go against the group even though we know in our hearts we are right.

As we look into these two abuses of spiritual power, we cannot help but notice how they play into each other in a very unhealthy way. The person who is the careless power broker often has all the power and none of the responsibility. In contrast, the powerless person has the responsibility for

99

everything, and is blamed when things go contrary to what the power broker wants. We do not need alcoholism and other illnesses in our families to have unhealthy relationships. Abuse of power can be just as destructive.

Using Our Own Spiritual Power

If spiritual power is so strong, then people can use it in an important way during the recovery process by setting interpersonal boundaries. We all impact others and they us. Hopefully, this will happen in a positive way through behaviors such as encouragement, support, and honesty. But too often this impact spills over into unhealthy behaviors such as using, manipulating, fixing, and overprotecting. We become entangled in being responsible for everyone else, but we are not responsible for ourselves.

The key to setting interpersonal boundaries is to prayerfully and consciously get a clear picture of what is our "baggage" and what belongs to others. Instead of trying to analyze and fix everyone else, we need to take our own spiritual inventory and get rid of our character defects with God's help. Instead of depending on everyone else for our sense of happiness and worth, we need to depend on God, our inner resources, and the support system our Lord gives us.

While we may be very clear about our interpersonal boundaries, other people may not. They may violate our boundaries by trying to figure us out, fix us, control us, interfere with our lives, or invade our privacy and personal space. With these people, we need to exercise spiritual power by clearly and assertively sharing our boundaries with them. If they continue to violate them we need to leave. This leaving may vary from taking a short walk to deciding to minimize or end that relationship.

Let's consider some guidelines for receiving and living with the spiritual power that God wants to give us:

First, spiritual power comes to us through humble prayer. We must admit our powerlessness and helplessness before God. Hardly anyone feels he or she can just admit their wrongdoings or surrender their pride, especially to God. When we realize our failures and powerlessness, we are actually taking a giant leap toward spiritual power and healing. In our prayers, we must be honest with God and honest with ourselves. That means recognizing the sin, the suffering and the barriers which affect our lives. In *The Art of Happiness*, the Dalai Lama shares this counsel:

> *If you directly confront your suffering, you will be in a better position to appreciate the depth and nature of the problem. If you are in a battle, as long as you remain ignorant of the status and combat ability of the enemy, you will be totally unprepared and paralyzed by your fear.* [p. 137]

Second, spiritual power grows as our intimacy with God also grows. The closer we are to God, the more we know of his love and power working together in our lives. We will often see circumstances coming together in a better way than we ever planned. And even when circumstances are refusing to come together, we trust that God's love and power are still working in our lives.

For this intimacy, we cannot simply know a lot about God. It isn't enough to know the Bible intellectually. We need to know God personally, vulnerably, and honestly. As Tim Hansel says: "Knowing in both the Old and New Testament implies intimacy, deep understanding, and experience. It implies an element of participation beyond mere cerebral assent. It is a belief which has matured and taken new root, and has been translated from mere cognition to a new kind of power."

Third, spiritual power must always be exercised unselfishly to do God's will, not ours. In all of his miracles, Jesus never once used spiritual power for self-centered motives. In fact, the theme of Satan's temptation in Matthew 4 was seeking to persuade Jesus to use his power for a selfish agenda. (Actually, it was Satan's selfish agenda.)

We must pray for knowledge of God's will. This requires an open mind and heart willing to discover any new possibility. We also need to pray for power to carry out His will. God never calls us to do anything that He does not equip us for.

Finally, spiritual power requires accountability. We need to be sure that all we say and do in God's name is accountable to the spirit of Jesus Christ and the Bible. We must be careful that we do not hand pick Scriptures that seem to justify us while ignoring the multitude of Scriptures that seek to dissuade us.

This process is usually not possible on our own. We must be accountable to others. We must be accountable to a spiritual director or mentor who will tell us if we seem to be going off in a strange, self-serving direction. We need to be accountable to a support group that knows our needs, hang-ups, and spiritual gifts. And we need to be accountable to the body of Christ. While we can constructively and lovingly disagree with a decision made by the church, we cannot and should not do anything that will tear down or divide the body of Christ.

Good news! We don't need to be helpless victims any more. God gives us all the spiritual power we need to change ourselves, set boundaries, and impact the world around us in a positive way.

Chapter 10
The Need to Serve Others

...whoever wishes to become great among
you must be your servant.   Mark 10:43

Bonnie grew up in an unhappy home. Her dad continually belittled her and tried to tell Bonnie how to do everything. When she did not follow every instruction to the tiniest detail, her father yelled at her and called her names. His treatment seemed even worse when compared to the favoritism he showed to Bonnie's older brother Bobby.

Bonnie felt little comfort from her mother. Her mom was often sick and depressed, so she abdicated her responsibility for household chores to Bonnie. The pressure robbed Bonnie of her childhood, and she became super-responsible in order to avoid feelings of worthlessness.

When Bonnie grew up, she married and had her own family. Her parents' health failed as they grew older, so Bonnie tried to take care of them. She took them on vacation with her, accompanied them to the doctor's office, and looked after them when they were sick. Of course, nothing Bonnie did seemed good enough for her father, and he continued to yell at her regularly.

Bonnie worked at a government agency where her supervisor was moody and insecure. While she often found him to be kind and supportive, he unpredictably sank into bad moods where he criticized and shouted at her. At work, Bonnie cringed with the same fear she experienced in her family.

Eventually, Bonnie's older brother Bobby contracted cancer. Because their parents were in poor health, Bonnie took care of him until he died. Not only did she blame herself for his death, but Bonnie also bore the full brunt of her father's wrath, which included a lot of anger over losing his son. It was impossible for her to please her father.

While it seems that Bonnie did many good things to serve others, there's another piece to this story. Bonnie usually did those things simply to avoid the discomfort of conflict. She believed her perfection could protect her from criticism. But she wasn't perfect, so when she was criticized, she was angry with herself and with others.

At this point, Bonnie went into a deep depression. She was restless, had difficulty sleeping, and cried uncontrollably. Her doctor referred her to a pastoral counselor. Since she had amassed a large amount of anger toward God, and authority figures in general, Bonnie went very reluctantly.

Her first words to the counselor were: "I don't like churches and I don't like preachers. I am here to deal with my depression. Nothing else!" The counselor respected her wishes and focused on her problems. In the counseling process, Bonnie grieved her brother, dealt with her anger toward her father, and learned to love herself. She also began to learn how much God loved her. Within a year, Bonnie was baptized and became an active member of a church.

Today, Bonnie is still a person who serves others. But now she does it for different reasons. She no longer serves in order to ease her own guilt and keep away all the criticism. She helps others because she is grateful for what God does for her. She no longer doubts her worth when people criticize her, but she loves others for who they are.

In this process, Bonnie took on a new attitude about her verbally abusive supervisor. Whenever the supervisor tore into her, Bonnie would go up to him, hug him, and tell him how much God loved him. She listened as he shared his woes with her. When Bonnie left that place of work, the supervisor wept. He felt like he was losing a kind and giving friend.

After some time, Bonnie's mother developed cancer, so Bonnie moved into her parents' home and tended to her mom. Meanwhile, her father continued to criticize everything she did. However, Bonnie did not cringe in terror. She held her ground, responding both kindly and firmly to her father's tirades. Her mother passed from this life feeling loved and protected by her caring daughter.

Bonnie showed her service and care in many friendships. One friend struggled with devastating family problems. Bonnie affirmed her, supported her, and helped her get the counseling she needed. Two of Bonnie's grandchildren required child care while their parents were at work, so she took on the job. She loved those children and delighted in showing them the birds, bugs, and other wonders of creation. Bonnie had a peculiar relative whom no one in the family liked. When this cousin grew terribly sick, she called him, prayed for him, and sent him cards. After his hospitalization, she took him into her home and took care of him.

Bonnie continues to do many small and beautiful works of serving others. When a friend is moving, she is there to help. When her family suffers a crisis, she is there. When the church sanctuary needs to be decorated for Easter, she pours out her love and artistic talents. Bonnie was transformed from feeling worthless and overly responsible to being a loving person who finds her greatest joy in helping others. Whereas she once did acts of kindness to avoid criticism and conflict, she now does them for positive reasons, growing out of her relationship with God and her love of others.

Jesus as Servant

Serving others seems to be the core interpersonal value in Jesus' life and teachings. He fully lived out the prophesied role of the Messiah who was the Suffering Servant in Isaiah 53. While he is the King of kings and Lord of lords, serving others is the key to his mission. He explained: "'the Son of Man came not to be served but to serve, and to give his life as a ransom for many'" (Matthew 20:28).

Jesus constantly tried to teach the same joyful service to his followers. He told them greatness did not come from power, authority, and control, but from doing humble acts of service for others. He told them to heal the sick, welcome children, and give a cup of cold water in his name.

Jesus used servanthood as the measure to determine those who had true faith and those who had no faith. In Matthew 25, he talks about dividing the sheep from the goats at the final judgment. Those who come into the kingdom are ones who fed the hungry, gave drink to the thirsty, welcomed strangers, clothed the naked, cared for the sick, and visited the prisoner. Those who were excluded from the kingdom failed to do these things. In fact, Jesus told us that acts of kindness done to others was the same as serving him.

Jesus' most profound teaching of servanthood came at the Last Supper when he washed the feet of his disciples (John 13:1-17). Wearing sandals and walking on dusty roads made for extremely dirty feet in those days. A good host would assign a slave to wash the feet of the guests as they came in. But there were no slaves at that Last Supper, and all the disciples were busy seeking a higher place in the kingdom (Luke 22:24-27). So there they sat around the table of the most memorable meal in history with stinky, dirty feet.

Jesus knew that simply teaching them about servanthood was not enough. He had to show them. So he rose, tied a towel around his waist, took a basin, knelt, and washed their feet. Embarrassed, Peter at first protested. But Jesus told him that being part of the kingdom involved both serving and being served. Jesus told them that they too must be servants: *"For I have set you an example, that you also should do as I have done for you"* (John 13:15).

Service in the Recovery Church

Service is one of the three basic keys of 12-step recovery programs. Alcoholics Anonymous speaks of recovery, unity, and service as the three legs of a triangle. Addicted people know they have become self-centered and self-absorbed in their disease. They know that serving others is the only antidote.

When newcomers arrive at a 12-step meeting, they are usually overwhelmed at the kindness. One stranger greets them while another offers a cup of coffee. They are told that being so new in the recovery process makes them the most important people present. They hear words of encouragement from members of the group who tell them to "keep coming back." After the meeting, members offer their support and even their telephone numbers to them. Often members of the group will receive telephone calls from these newcomers in the middle of the night or other inopportune times. Still, group members will drop everything to go and help the newcomer.

Why do members do this? Because they remember it was done for them when they first came into the recovery program. They also use service to counterattack the self-centeredness that almost destroyed them. Such service is given without the expectation of anything in return. The AA saying "Pass It On" is all about this philosophy.

Parenthetically, the church could learn a lot from 12-step programs on how to welcome newcomers. Can you imagine what would happen to the life and the growth of the body of Christ if we treated our newcomers the same way? You may wish to read the book *Widening the Welcome of Your Church* by Fred Bernhard and Steve Clapp, which talks about ways for congregations to better demonstrate hospitality to all who come.

Members of 12-step programs sometimes fall back into self-absorption and self-centeredness. They get lost in their own thoughts and their own problems so much that they lose track of the world, life, and people around them. At these times, they are most prone to relapse into their addiction. In fact, whenever a member has a strong urge to relapse, the group gives the same advice: Get out of your own head. They are told, when all else fails, to work with another alcoholic! Helping another person can revitalize your own life. Serving others is a key element of recovery and of the Christian life. As we receive healing, we need to show the same kindness to others. Service should be given freely without selfish intentions.

What recovery means is not just overcoming one's addictions but discovering and living out our higher purpose in life–in other words, not just surviving but thriving! We need to practice the words of Paul: "(God) consoles us in all our affliction, so that we may be able to console those who are in any affliction with the consolation with which we ourselves are consoled by God" (2 Corinthians 1:4).

Many people believe that we find happiness by getting things for ourselves. The more power and control we have, the more we get, and the happier we will be. But those of us who have experimented in that direction can tell you that this is not true.

Kingdom servanthood tells us to be as caring with others as we are with ourselves. Jesus says we will only find meaning in life if we are willing to give up ourselves (Matthew 10:39). We have the most impact on this world, not by seeking secular power and control, but by serving others. Worldly possessions are meaningless compared with what we possess in God's kingdom. Happiness comes from giving, not getting.

How to Begin a Life of Service

There are four helpful guidelines in considering a lifestyle of helping others:

First, serving others frees us from self. When we become obsessed with ourselves, our happiness, our wants, our problems, our loneliness, and our struggles, we are usually unhappy. But when we get out of ourselves and give to those in need, this unhappiness disappears. To find the joy of being, we need to experience the joy of doing for others.

Happiness has a way of eluding us when we pursue it as a goal. The world of advertising tries to convince us that we can find happiness in the home we own, the car we drive, the clothes we wear, or the vacation we take. But there is no guarantee that any of those will make us happy. When we focus on living the right kind of life and on reaching out to others, we find that happiness comes to us even though we are not directly seeking it.

Second, serving others needs to be done with the proper motivation. Our motivation for helping others should not be to ease our guilt, prove our worth, earn our salvation, or make others like us. We need to serve because we have received so much. Out of our gratitude for what we are given, we cannot help but give to others. Jesus said, "Freely you have received, freely give'" (Matthew 10:8).

Third, serving others takes no special talents, skills, training, or experience. The things that Jesus told us to do, such as feeding the hungry, welcoming the stranger, and visiting the sick, require no special skills at all. Anyone can serve!

Last, we need to begin to serve where we are right now. We should not wait for a vision to show us some place to serve halfway around the world. We need to open our spiritual eyes and see the needs of others around us. Often it involves seemingly insignificant acts. But the simple actions matter most to God.

In 1999, for example, Sam was between pastorates and had time for reflection and healing. No longer was he committed to "important" acts of service like preaching a sermon, visiting someone with terminal cancer, or helping a hurting person find recovery and salvation. Instead of giving in to feelings of worthlessness, however, he began to look around at what needed to be done. He began to serve by making the bed, fixing supper, or doing laundry. Sam found that God treasured these acts of service just as much, perhaps even more, than all the other "important" things he had done. He rediscovered the joy of simple service.

Ways to Serve God Through Others

There are a number of venues of service for those in a spiritual program of recovery and for all those involved in the life of the Christian community. We can start with the ones closest to us and gradually move in additional directions.

We can serve our partners and families. Families are unhealthy when one person does all the giving, and another all the taking. Husbands and wives need to both seek opportunities to be helpful and kind. It is important to be a supportive *friend* to one's partner and not view what we do for each other as marital obligations.

We can serve our children and ask for them to help us. For example, parents can be active in their schooling through help with homework or as a volunteer in the PTA. In turn, children can learn about the work their parents do when they are not home; and children can take responsibility for some household tasks. Children need to be taught how to care and how to be responsible, instead of having every want or need met.

Some people who live together are friends rather than husband and wife. Many households have a single parent. Persons who live alone nevertheless have close bonds with at least some other people. Whatever the family structure, it's important to seek opportunities to serve those with whom we share our lives.

In the entire family, we can listen, encourage, laugh, cry, and struggle with one another. We can spend time along with our partners and families without any entertainment, allowing us to discover new insights about one another. Together we can study the Bible, take up a new family hobby, take more vacations, and volunteer in the community. Learning and living out the lessons life has to teach us as a family can bring immense joy and better relationships.

We can serve our support group. A support group can be any kind of group where two or more share and listen to the struggles of others without judgment, condemnation, or interruption. A support group can meet to heal personal emotional problems or discuss social dilemmas. Examples of support groups can be a women's or men's group; Bible study group; a workplace support group; a grandparents' group; or simply any group that is open to discussion and willing to provide love and understanding to each of the participants.

In a support group we can pray for the needs of others on a daily basis. We can set up tables and chairs, bring refreshments, and serve as a greeter. We can welcome and even sponsor the newcomer. We can serve as a volunteer or leader. We can offer hope by sharing our own experience, strength, and faith with others. We can be good friends to others. The key objective to any kind of support group is *growth,* whether it be social, emotional, mental, physical, or especially spiritual. No matter what is discussed, a support group is healthy and successful when its members experience some kind of personal change or fulfillment.

We can serve our church. We can serve on committees, teach Sunday School, or sing in the choir. We can volunteer time for church projects or visit the sick and shut-ins. We can become greeters and ushers, participate in or lead youth activities, begin a pre-school or adult day care, start a homeless shelter or food pantry, serve as a missionary at home or abroad, or start a new ministry outreach in the community. God has given us special spiritual gifts. We must discern what they are and then use them for the good of God and others.

Encourage the pastor and other leaders. Pastors and church leaders seldom receive all the support they need. We often view the pastor as having a solid grip on all church events and organizational priorities, but many pastors feel overwhelmed with a multitude of responsibilities. We can help them out by picking up some tasks and encouraging them to take personal time. The pastor and other church leaders need emotional and spiritual support. For a more detailed discussion on ways to help the pastor be healthier and more effective, read *Healthy Pastor–Healthy Church* by Joan Hershey and Steve Clapp.

We can serve in our communities. Sports leagues need coaches. Nursing homes have lonely people who hunger for company. Community cleanup and building projects need volunteers. Scouts need leaders. Abused children need safe, supportive adults in their lives. People new to the community need friends and someone to show them around. Kids need mentors to help them deal with peer pressures.

We can also help develop or support local public policy, whether it be for better schools, housing, or environment. We can organize community initiatives to improve the safety of the neighborhoods. We can write to prisoners to offer personal support and to lawmakers to improve our judicial system. We can stop finding fault with where we live and start working to make it a better place.

Finally, we can serve in our world. Refugees need food, clothing, and other basic necessities. Habitat for Humanity needs workers all over the world to help build housing for needy people. Disaster areas need volunteers to help with the cleanup and rebuilding. Work projects and service projects in inner cities and third world countries need participants. Missionaries need supplies, prayers, and letters from home.

We can learn more about social and political issues around the world and how those issues affect individuals and particular groups of people. We can become advocates of human rights that affect every nation of the world. Or we can simply be a part of expanding the knowledge and friendship of other nations by creating a network of supportive pen-pals for both kids and adults.

No matter who, where, or how we serve, it is all done for Jesus. Thus, there is no greater joy!

Chapter Eleven
The Need to Carry the Message

> *This saying is sure and worthy of full acceptance,*
> *that Christ Jesus came into the world to save sinners-*
> *of whom I am the foremost. But for that very reason I*
> *received mercy, so that in me, as the foremost, Jesus*
> *Christ may display the utmost patience, making me an*
> *example to those who would come to believe in Him for*
> *eternal life.*   1 Timothy 1:15-16

With her bouts of severe depression and strong suicidal thoughts, everyone, including Judy herself, thought she was crazy. Her emotional vulnerability left her unable to keep a job. She went to many therapists and took the gamut of psychiatric medications, but her problems continued. She lived with an older man named Jim who verbally abused her. Judy's children were afraid to let her care for her grandchildren because they felt she was insane and feared her.

But Judy wasn't crazy. She was highly dysfunctional, but not crazy. Her instability grew out of the family in which she grew up. Judy was the oldest of four children growing up in a blue-collar family. Her father was an alcoholic who verbally and sexually abused her. On top of that, Judy's mother enabled this molestation. Whenever Judy did something to disappoint them, she was punished by being forced to sleep with her father. Her siblings were all treated more fairly, while Judy was the family scapegoat and was blamed for everything.

As Judy became an adult, she began to suppress the memories of the abuse and developed defense mechanisms in order to survive emotionally. She married an alcoholic (like her father) who was also abusive to her. Together they had three children. Judy finally divorced her husband after her children were grown. Because of her inability to make it on her own, she quickly moved in with Jim.

After going through all kinds of ineffective treatments, she was referred by her family physician to a Christian counselor. The counselor refused to believe that Judy was crazy and helped Judy recognize how dysfunctional her family had been. She repeatedly assured Judy, "You are not crazy, but your family was."

Through counseling, the memories of her sexual abuse came back to her. She shared them with her counselor and, in the process, started to let go of the anger, guilt, and shame. She began to stand up to people who used to treat her like a doormat. She even stood up to Jim and insisted he join her in counseling.

There was a strong spiritual component in Judy's recovery. She attended meetings of Al-Anon (for family members of alcoholics) and became active in a local church. Her counselor consistently reinforced the idea that Judy was a precious child of God, special in His eyes. She wasn't bad or "crazy." Judy began to live more in God's love and worried less about what people thought of her. Whenever "crazy" feelings came to her, she learned to turn them over to God.

But that's only half of Judy's story. While life for her was still a struggle in many respects, she became filled with gratitude for her ongoing recovery. Within six months, she invited three friends to Al-Anon and to church. Because of her tremendous excitement, they all came. She also invited members of her family to church. Judy, her son, one of her sisters, and two of her friends were all baptized the same day.

Meanwhile, Jim felt left out. He was frightened by the changes in Judy, but he agreed to go to counseling with her. She realized he was just going through the motions so she decided to leave him. Jim then realized how much he loved and missed her. He earnestly became involved in counseling, attending church, and developing a relationship with God. He spent long hours in prayer surrendering himself to God's will. Within six months, Judy and Jim were married.

Judy impacted the lives of at least six other people by encouraging them to participate in recovery and in church. Today she shares the message of hope and recovery by continuing to invite new people. Other's lives are changed because Judy successfully carries the message to those she loves. She expressed her passions in this poem:

> *We all need each other,*
> *to work together, to love*
> *and cherish our helpless*
> *brother who is in need.*
> *We come together for whatever*
> *it takes to fix someone in need.*
>
> *So let's rise above all the sorrow*
> *and turn this world around.*
> *Turn it around for something good.*
> *Make people stand up and cheer.*
> *You will become a hero, you will*
> *become a knight in bright colors.*

(A word of caution. In this book, stories have been shared about the positive experiences people have had working with Christian counselors. These are trained counselors who integrate their understanding of the Christian faith into their efforts to help people improve their lives. In selecting a counselor, it is very important to seek referral from someone whose judgment you trust. You should not automatically conclude a counselor will be good because he or she has the adjective "Christian" attached to his or her title. Some persons who call themselves Christian counselors have very little professional training. Likewise, there are many counselors who do not label themselves Christian who nevertheless have deep respect for the spiritual dimension of life.)

Carrying the Message

Probably the foremost biblical example of "carrying the message" can be found in the story of Philip and Nathaniel in John 1:43-51. After discovering Jesus, Philip sought out his friend Nathaniel because Philip understood his spiritual void and hunger. Even so, Nathaniel doubted the message of Jesus and argued theologically with his friend. Rather than being drawn into fruitless debate, Philip offered the ultimate invitation: "Come and see" (John 1:46).

115

Nathaniel finally agreed to meet this mysterious man from Nazareth. As Nathaniel heard Jesus speak directly to him about his spiritual hunger, Nathaniel's faith allowed him to believe in Jesus' message. Philip did not force Nathaniel to convert but merely introduced him to Jesus, where true conversion by his grace alone took place.

This passage has some truth to tell us about evangelism and "carrying the message." It tells us that sharing what God has done for us is at the heart of caring friendship. It also tells us that theological debates have little to do with the conversion experience. Our task as witnesses is to introduce people to Jesus and let him do the rest.

In writing to Timothy, Paul further illustrated this humble, sharing approach to evangelism. Because of his widespread influence over both Jews and Gentiles, Paul could very well have gained followers with an attitude of personal superiority. Christ appeared to him in a spectacular vision, and he was hand-picked specifically by God to be an "apostle to the Gentiles." But in his witness, Paul refused to come from such a superior position. He publicly proclaimed that he was the worst of sinners and that God had shown remarkable patience and mercy to one such as he.

Paul was successful in reaching people for God not only because he had a deep understanding of theology and spirituality, but because he had a true love for God. His emphasis was not upon how wonderful or special he was. In his joy and passion, he wanted everyone to receive the wonderful gift of eternal life in Jesus Christ.

In 12-step programs, "carrying the message" is clearly defined in Step Twelve: *Having had a spiritual awakening as a result of these steps, we tried to carry the message. . . and to practice these principles in all our affairs.* People in recovery will go to others in response to their request for help, whether it comes from the one seeking recovery or a family member of that person.

At the same time, it is not appropriate to "preach" to others about their sins or addictions. People in recovery should simply tell their stories and hope the listener desires assistance. Giving the person freedom to reject the offer still "leaves the door open" to be of future assistance when he or she feels it's time.

116

As for the church's role in carrying the message, openness to people in recovery is an excellent way to reach many people who have no church connection. These are sometimes described as "wandering Christians," because they go from church to church, seeking a meaningful connection. Many church growth experts also agree, including Edwin Bontrager who writes in *Following the Footsteps of Paul*: "Over 70 percent of those looking for a church are codependent, addicted or dysfunctional" [pp. 48-49].

Understanding Evangelism

So how do we reach those who may be in recovery or simply need spiritual help without unintentionally turning them away? Let's take a closer look at the concept of evangelism.

The word "evangelism" has come to mean negative things in some congregations. In a few it has lost its original intent of "bringing the good news." Some understand it as preaching, accosting strangers on the street, or forcing our beliefs on others. As a result of these misunderstandings, many churches nationwide face dwindling church attendance, and some congregations are dying.

One of the core problems is that many of our churches do not offer training or orientation in how to go about sharing the faith. Christian Community and LifeQuest conducted a study in 1995, 1996, and 2000 examining attitudes and practices of active congregational members in local churches which are growing in contrast to those which are staying the same in membership or declining.

Among other things, persons in the study were asked to indicate if they had received some kind of instruction from the church in how to share their faith with others and in how to invite others to worship and other church events. The striking difference is shown on the following chart. Members in churches which are growing were more than six times as likely to have received instruction in faith-sharing as those in churches which are declining.

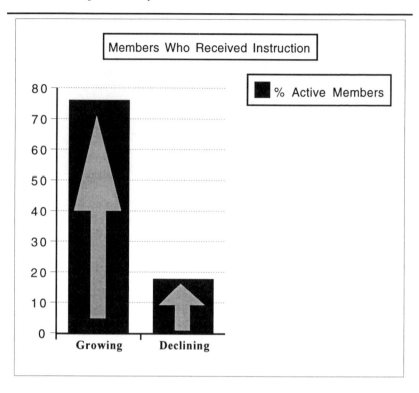

Let's examine some of the common distortions of the word "evangelism." **First, sometimes people, often with good intentions, approach the task of evangelism from a superior position.** Some believe that they have all the answers to salvation and grace and that those who are not in the church are ignorant. They believe they are the saints, while the others are sinners. They believe their task is to make the others similar to themselves. Ego and pride are often the main culprits behind these distortions. Those who are approached sense a condescending attitude and reject the faith which is offered.

The second distortion of evangelism comes when we make faith-sharing an intellectual exercise. Unlike Middle Eastern cultures, out of which Christianity was born, Western society places especially great importance on intellectual approaches to life. Some people interpret evangelism as simply bringing the other person to a point of intellectual agreement with their positions. It's even possible to intellectually recognize the existence of Christ but still fail to enter a living relationship with him. But the Bible warns against this: "You believe that God is one; you do well. Even the demons believe and shudder" (James 2:19).

While reason and logic certainly can play an important part in helping a person be open to the possibility of God's existence and claim on one's life, the heart of evangelism is in trust and faith–trust in the person who shares the good news and then faith in God who is the good news. Successful evangelism is not about intellectual fulfillment. Teaching people biblical truths is not the primary goal of evangelism. It follows one's personal expression of faith in Christ. The main purpose of evangelism is to create a conducive climate in which people can and want to accept a life-changing relationship with God and his people.

Relationship, not intellectual ideas, is key. We can know a lot about God, but until we know God personally, it does us little good. Our love for God is best demonstrated in our covenant relationship with other believers. If we cause division and strife in the church community, the love of God is not in us. Jesus said, "'By this everyone will know that you are my disciples, if you have love for one another'" [John 13:35]. Filled with God's love, we want to share what we have discovered with others.

A third common distortion in the understanding of evangelism in our time comes from assuming that all those outside the church do not believe in God or in Christ. In contemporary North America, that is not a valid assumption. Polls continually show that by far the majority of people who are not members of a church nevertheless believe in God, pray on a frequent basis, and self-identify as Christian. More of the people outside the church have rejected the church itself than have rejected God. When we approach those who are not in the church on the assumption that they have no beliefs of importance, we insult them and almost guarantee that they will not listen to us. People have become disillusioned with the institutional church for a variety of reasons, some of which are valid and some of which are not. Consider the following factors:

- Some persons who did not grow up in a family which was church active have had almost no exposure to

119

the Christian community. Thus they really do not understand well either the strengths or weaknesses of congregational life.

- Some persons who grew up in the church had very negative experiences. The church may have been overly strict or judgmental toward them. That was the case for Elizabeth, whose story is shared in Chapter Nine.

- Some persons have been the victims of gossip within the Christian community or have felt that their opinions and beliefs were not respected by others. Having had such experiences, they are reluctant to try again.

- Some persons are turned off by what they see as the slowness of churches to change. They see many congregations reluctant to try new music or alternatives to the sermon like video or drama. They are frustrated because it takes so many meetings and so much discussion for many congregations to make decisions. They do not recognize that some churches are different.

- Some people avoid the church because they feel that their lifestyle would not be accepted. This can include male and female couples who live together but are not married and persons of homosexual orientation. This can also include people who struggle with addictions such as alcoholism.

Those factors and more can keep people who believe in God from wanting contact with the institutional church. When we seek to share the faith with others and to invite others to become involved in the church, we need to be aware that the issue may be a rejection of the church rather than a rejection of God.

Beggars of the Truth

Probably the best description of evangelism is from D.T. Niles: "Evangelism is one beggar telling another beggar where to find bread." We need to understand that we are beggars. We continue to recognize that we are in desperate need of God's mercy. We have accomplished nothing on our own. God did it all for us. We are people, born with sin, growing out of our pain into God's healing. We have not yet arrived. We are still on the journey.

We also need to understand the spiritual hunger of those we share spiritual food with. If our neighbor's children were emaciated and starving to death, we would be the first to bring them some food. But spiritual starvation, which is less visible, is just as deadly. We need to understand their pain and hunger before we can give them what they really need. We have to listen and care before we share our faith with them. This gives our faith-sharing a power beyond our understanding.

What is our witness to others? It comes not from our strength but from our weakness. Roy Oswald, senior consultant for the Alban Institute, said, "Our gift comes out of our struggle." From this, we understand three things which are important as we share our faith with others.

We need to share our *experiences*. We must show how God has helped us in the past. We must tell the other person about our own struggles and how God helped us to overcome them. In sharing our experience, the other person can often see a mirror image of his or her own struggles. People are far more likely to identify with our struggles and our weakness than with our strength.

We need to share *our strength*. Our strength is not our personal strength, but how God makes a difference in our lives every day. It's important to share how God has helped us in the past, but we also need to share how God is helping us in the present. We can talk about God's love as a never-ending resource in dealing with our ongoing struggles, which is a message of great importance to persons who struggle with recovery issues or with other areas of brokenness in their lives.

As we talk about the ways in which God has helped us, we also need to help people understand that God is not simply a tool to be used to cope with life. While God is more than willing to help us with our addictions, our loneliness, our insecurity, and our troubled relationships, he wants to be at the center of our lives–not simply a source of help in times of trouble. *The whole of life, properly understood for the Christian, is not about achieving our own happiness or fulfilling our own needs but about placing God at the center of our existence and letting that relationship affect every decision that we make.* When we let Christ take control of our lives, then we receive blessings beyond measure–though Christ may take us in directions we do not expect to go.

We need to share our *hope*. God has not only helped us in the past. He is not just with us in the present. He is with us in our future. We hear and trust his promises, including the promise of eternal life. God alone gives true purpose and direction to our lives. We are freed from worry and fear about the future because we trust God will always be there.

Most of us are not going to share all three of those perspectives in a single conversation They should be carefully and sensitively divulged over a period of time in the context of friendship. It usually takes more than one conversation, and usually more than one person, for someone to open up to a life-changing relationship with God and the Christian community.

Many have felt neglected in their suffering, even by well-meaning Christians. They are turned off by the church, organized religion and perhaps even their own perceptions of God. When this happens, we should not fall into the trap of offering excuses and justifications. Instead, we should listen compassionately to their expression of pain. We must carefully and sensitively show them a more compassionate and biblical God.

Carrying the message does not stop once the person we share our faith with enters into a relationship with God. Even when they have accepted Christ and are involved in a church, our job has just begun. We are friends, and friendship does not stop with conversion. We need to help them work all the biblical steps of recovery, not just the "sinner's prayer" offered at the altar. We need to remember that addiction is not a sin, but a disease. While sinful behavior may come out of the addiction, the addiction itself should never be considered a sin. We need to remember that the Great Commission does not merely call us to make Christians but to make disciples [Matthew 28:19].

As we discussed in our book *Sharing Living Water*, a couple of cautions are important. We must approach others with genuine respect. "Soul respects another's failure to find perfection, resistance to enlightenment, sheer ignorance of absolute truth, misguided attachments, and unrelenting meandering" [p. 30]. It's not our goal to manipulate anyone or to do anything obnoxious.

Thomas Moore, in *Meditations*, shares this perspective: "I've never had the impression that Jesus or the Buddha were proselytizers. It simply wasn't their style to run membership campaigns or even to 'network'" [p. 30]. It's extremely important to respect the right of others to see the world differently than we do and to express their beliefs differently than we choose to do. We are called to share the faith we have received; we are not called to impose it.

Another caution: our motivation for sharing our faith must be something other than or at least more than the church being in trouble. Many of our churches are in trouble in terms of membership, attendance, volunteer workers, and finances–but rescuing the church is not the best reason to reach out to others. Perhaps God has in fact decided to use the decline in many of our churches as an opportunity to motivate us to share our faith and do what we should have been doing all along. Living water is meant to be shared–not to be hoarded. Faith–sharing at its best, by God's grace, is an experience of mutuality from which both parties gain.

In *Sharing Living Water*, we suggested the following as an overall strategy for sharing our faith:

We can comfortably relate our faith in Christ to others and invite others into the life of the church through a process of:

- *Forming genuine friendships.*

- *Listening to the needs of our friends and learning to ask deeper questions.*

- *Caring for our friends and showing that care in words and actions.*
- *Telling in our own words how Christ and the church have made a difference in our lives, building not so much on our strength or wisdom as on our weakness.*

- *Inviting others into the life of the congregation.*

- *Helping those who join the church become fully incorporated into the body of Christ.*

- *Recognizing that it is Christ who saves and that we must respect where others are in openness to Christ and the church.*

There is probably no better way to grow in what God has given us than by sharing it with others. Carrying the message to hurting people furthers our own healing, increases our passion and devotion, and gives us the hope that we can conquer all things.

Chapter Twelve
Building Bridges

> *For we each are God's servants,*
> *working together; you are God's field,*
> *God's building.* 1 Corinthians 3:9

Gilbert Romero has served as the pastor of the Bella Vista Church of the Brethren in East Los Angeles for the past 15 years. While his life as a pastor has brought much joy and fulfillment to others as well as himself, he struggled with problems of addiction for most of his early years.

Gilbert was raised in a dysfunctional home in East Los Angeles. Because his father was never home, he never received the warmth and love that a father and son should share. He was told to be seen and not heard. He was not allowed to have fun as a child and spent a lot of time working. Both his father and his mother were sexually unfaithful to each other, and Gilbert had many half-brothers and sisters–but did not realize it until he was an adult.

Gilbert's mother died when he was 12 years old. He was placed in a foster home at that time for trying to kill his father. At this age, Gilbert began experimenting with drugs such as "bennies" and inhalants. His lack of a real home life led to his involvement in a gang. By age 13, he was addicted to heroin and heavily into drinking. He spent most of his time in and out of jails, treatment facilities, county homes, and various custodies. Because his life felt meaningless, Gilbert overdosed on drugs when he was 14. While he survived the experience, he spent many years living on the street. He was arrested numerous times for driving under the influence and was involved in traffic accidents with injuries.

Due to his serious problems associated with drinking, a judge finally sentenced him to attend 50 meetings of Alcoholics

Anonymous in six months. Naturally, Gilbert put off attending AA meetings until two weeks were left. He met with the judge and was told he now had to attend 50 AA meetings in two weeks. He hit every AA meeting he could find and reached the 50-meeting mark before the two weeks were up.

But something significant happened to Gilbert at these AA meetings. He started to hear what he needed to hear. He began to admit he had a problem. For the first time, he started to make real friends. Someone gave him the books *Alcoholics Anonymous* and *Twelve Steps and Twelve Traditions*. He devoured the books, learning much about himself in the process. Gilbert took an honest look at himself and his addiction. He admitted that his life was out of control.

When Gilbert was 28 years old, he met his wife. They fell in love but both still had problems with addiction. Dutifully, Gilbert went to Debbie's grandparents and asked permission to marry her. They recognized his struggle with addiction but didn't kick him out. Instead, they invited him in to live with them. They were strong Christian people who offered prayers, love, and support as they helped Gilbert deal with his personal issues.

While living with this family, Gilbert attended church services as well as AA and Narcotics Anonymous meetings. He allowed God to take charge of his life, praying that he would see results within one year. Within five months of attending church and 12-step meetings, his desire to use drugs was taken away. He was touched by the Holy Spirit. To this day, Gilbert continues to see a counselor and attend a Christian 12-step meeting.

Gilbert began to integrate his recovery with his Christian faith. He continually invited people off the streets to live in his home, offering them recovery and Jesus Christ. He attempted to set up a halfway house for women, and he was able to persuade the Bella Vista church to have their old parsonage turned into a halfway house for men.

In the halfway house, men are required to work certain jobs, attend Bible study and 12-step meetings, and participate in church. Every Sunday morning, the men clean the church from top to bottom. Many are involved in jobs and some have gone to other churches across the country to help with recovery and

Hispanic ministries. Some of the men are afraid to go out on the streets because a rival gang has targeted them for trouble. The church property is the only place they feel safe.

After three years of recovery, Gilbert felt God's call to the pastoral ministry. When a pastoral position became available at Bella Vista, he was hired for the job. He still continues serving this church. Gilbert hosts a lively worship service filled with contemporary music and dynamic preaching. Not only has this once troubled church truly come to life, but he also continues his outreach ministry.

Gilbert has helped over 1,200 men and women through the halfway house program in East Los Angeles, but his ministry has not stopped there. His church is heavily involved with an orphanage in Tiajuana, Mexico with a ministry for homeless refugees in that country. Gilbert volunteers much time for his denomination by speaking in other churches, serving on the national board, and helping with church camps. He received the gifts of recovery and salvation, and he loves to pass them on.

The Need for Recovery

Recovery people meet in the basements and fellowship halls of churches all across the country. Those of us who have not been part of a 12-step group often know little about them, and we may even be disturbed by their presence and upset about the cigarette butts we find outside the building. But the reality is that God has placed many recovering people in our midst. Recovery ministry and "12-step spirituality" are knocking at the doors of our churches, presenting us an opportunity for outreach ministry. We cannot ignore this chance to bring others closer to Jesus.

Addictions to substances and habits have incredible impact both on those who suffer from the addiction and on those who are close to them. Let's take a closer look at alcohol and tobacco use by young people, for example. While the rate of cigarette smoking has decreased for older adults, there is an increase in smoking for youth aged 15-19 [Report on "Smoking Prevalence in Canada," 1999, and the American Lung Association, 2001]. More than a third of all high school students in the U.S. (34.8%) reported using some form of tobacco in the past month; about a quarter (28.4%) are currently regular smokers (National Youth Tobacco Survey, 1999). According to the American Lung Association, little progress has been made in stopping young adults and kids from smoking (2001).

In addition, about 38% of twelfth graders reported using marijuana (which has also experienced a resurgence among younger teens) and 62% of them reported having been drunk at least once. Every day people use illicit drugs, alcohol or cigarettes for the first time: 2,280 use marijuana, 4,213 drink alcohol, and 3,044 smoke cigarettes (National Clearinghouse for Alcohol and Drug Information, 1999; National Institute on Drug Abuse, 2000). These disturbing trends show that many young people are very susceptible to developing addictions.

Alcohol and smoking can easily be abused by just about anyone, and they can cause both a private disease for the person who uses them and a social illness for those who care very deeply for that person. Second-hand smoke affects people who do not even know the smoker, and people who have never touched a drink can be killed by a driver who is intoxicated. Everyone is affected, either directly or indirectly, by addictions such as these. While you yourself may not be experiencing the power of an addiction, you most likely know someone who does.

And then there are the more socially acceptable addictions to money and work which have been discussed earlier in this book. We can also become addicted to unhealthy sexual fixations, judgmentalism toward other people, and procrastination which keeps us from accomplishing what we should with our lives.

The gospel of Jesus Christ is empty without a focus on reaching out to those in need. Indeed, Jesus began his own ministry by quoting these words from Isaiah: "'The Spirit of the Lord is upon me, because he has anointed me to bring good news. He has sent be me to proclaim release to the captives and recovery of sight to the blind, to let the oppressed go free'" (Luke 4:18). People needing recovery are poor physically, emotionally and spiritually. They need to have their eyes opened and be freed from their compulsive behaviors and addictions.

The Gospel clearly tells us that the church needs to be open to all kinds of ministry. Ministry is not just done one way with one purpose. The good news of the Gospel is multifaceted. But sometimes sincere Christians feel their particular focus and method of ministry is the only valid one. As a result, we may ignore, exclude or unfairly condemn someone who does something differently.

Some focus on the "spiritual" ministry of "saving souls." Others focus on more "earthly" ministries such as working with homeless people, helping refugees, and championing social causes. Both of these aspects are valid parts of Christian ministry and would be more effective if they were integrated.

Jesus' disciples became jealous and critical of someone who was driving out demons in Jesus' name but was not part of their group. They asked Jesus to stop him because he was not one of them. Jesus responded: *"Do not stop him, for no one who does a deed of power in my name will be able soon afterward to speak evil of me. Whoever is not against us is for us"* (Mark 9:39-40). In recovery ministries, evangelical, charismatic, conservative, mainline, Catholic, and social justice churches have reached out and successfully transformed lives. All are involved in sharing God's plan of salvation.

The ministry of offering salvation takes many forms. But as Paul affirms in this chapter's opening Scripture: *We are God's servants, working together. . .* No matter how diverse our ministries, our forms of worship, and even our theology, we are still God's servants working together. Furthermore, Paul affirms our unity by saying that we *are God's field, God's building.* We are all working together on the same harvest. We are all building the same church.

Recovery ministry is not the only valid way of spreading the gospel, but in many circles it has been a neglected and ignored means. Recovery ministry brings many good things to the church, including deeper spirituality, new members with special spiritual gifts, and a valid and caring way to share the good news. The gap between the traditional church and the recovery community should not exist because both are based on the Gospel. It is time for churches to bridge the gap.

Building Bridges to Recovery in the Church

We would like to suggest four ways we can bridge this gap: increasing our awareness; making our churches more user-friendly; reaching out in the community to those in need; and establishing recovery ministries within the church.

First, we can raise the awareness of people in the church on the importance of recovery and the recognition that the principles of recovery can help all of us. We've intentionally included a study guide at the back of this book to make this a resource which can be used by Sunday school classes, small groups, church boards, and evangelism committees. Another wonderful resource is the videotape curriculum developed out of Keith Miller's book *Hunger for Healing*.

We can also stock our church libraries and encourage members to read books on Christian recovery. Some suggestions are offered in Chapter Eight in the discussion of study. Pastors and church leaders are urged to teach and preach on recovery themes. The truths in recovery spirituality help people with all kinds of problems, not just addiction. We need to do more than simply have support groups in the church made up of people in recovery. We need these people in our churches in order to share with them a life-giving message and to learn from them.

Second, we can make our churches more *user-friendly*. The primary way new people are introduced to our churches is through the worship service. Yet many newcomers find our services stale, lifeless, or irrelevant to everyday concerns. This is why many church visitors never come back. Music, the words we use, themes, and sermons can play key roles in making worship user-friendly.

Sam's sponsor has often told his church that the music reminds him of a funeral. He continually pleads for more lively, joy-filled music. While the church plays many beautiful hymns, a steady diet of them can be boring to some people. It has been estimated that 80 percent of the people in our society listen to contemporary music, while only 3 percent listen to classical music. Yet out of attachment to tradition, we opt for the classical flavor of traditional hymns instead of the kind of music to which our society relates. To solve this problem, many churches have opted for two services: one traditional and one contemporary. However, smaller churches who are not ready for two services need the tolerance and open-mindedness to use all kinds of music to celebrate Jesus Christ.

For instance, some people may not like country music. But because the main concern is to reach as many people with the healing of Christ as possible, we should be willing to use country or any type of non-traditional music in worship if that will attract more people to stay in the church. Personal likes and dislikes in music are a secondary concern to the priority of the Great Commission.

Being careful of the words we choose is another way to make our churches more user-friendly. The religious terms we use to express our faith to the unchurched and the broader community seem like a   foreign language. Words like "justification" and "sanctification" are not readily understood by those outside the Christian community–and not by all persons in that community. We can easily dispense with theological jargon and explain the principles of God's grace in words people understand.

Another opportunity to make our worship services more user-friendly can be found in our themes and sermons. Pastors need to remember the distinction between spirituality and theology in preparing sermons.   Many Christian or non-Christian newcomers to a church may not understand the basic tenets of the Methodist Church under John Wesley or the history of Alexander Mack with the Church of the Brethren. *Spirituality is having a healthy, dynamic and growing relationship with God, self, and others.* Our messages need to help lonely, hurting people find hope and healing.

Third, we can learn to reach out to addicted and hurting people in our communities. There are many ways we can do this. We can take leftovers from our potlucks to local halfway houses. With the help of Prison Fellowship, we can get involved in jail and prison ministries. We can offer counseling for individuals and families, day care for single mothers, food banks for needy people, and Bible studies on marriage and family.

Fourth, we can build a bridge between the church and recovery by developing specific recovery ministries within

the church. This opportunity is not right for every congregation, but it is an important option for many. There are many resources for these kinds of ministries. One is a quarterly magazine called *Steps* which comes from an organization called National Association for Christian Recovery. This magazine is full of informative articles to help us understand people with addictions or other recovery issues. They list resources for clergy, mental health professionals, and for Christians in general. They also list addresses and telephone numbers for a wide range of 12-step programs. The NACR Resource Center offers Recovery Bibles, Bible study materials, books, 12-step resources, and audio tapes. The address and telephone number for NACR are:

> National Association for Christian Recovery
> P.O. Box 215
> Brea, CA 92822-0215
> (714) 529-NACR (6227)

The second resource we recommend is a recovery curriculum called *Celebrate Recovery*. *Celebrate Recovery* was founded at the Saddleback Church in Lake Forest, California by John Baker. He developed it out of both his commitment to Jesus Christ and his own involvement in recovery. This program is not just for so-called "addicts" but for anyone with hurts, hang-ups, or habits they want to overcome. This opens Christ-centered recovery principles and spirituality to all Christians. In the leadership manual, John Baker writes:

> *The purpose of. . .* Celebrate Recovery *is to fellowship and celebrate God's healing power in our lives through eight recovery principles and the Christ-centered 12 steps. . . By working the steps and applying their Biblical principles, we begin to grow spiritually.   We become free from our addictive, compulsive, and dysfunctional behaviors. This freedom creates peace, serenity, joy, and most importantly, a strong personal relationship with God and others.* [p 221]

The starter kit includes the leader's manual, set of four workbooks, a video tape promotion of the program, audio tapes, and computer guides to both the sermon manuscripts and the small group teaching curriculum. Celebrate Recovery materials can be ordered from:

pastors.com
www.pastors.com
949-829-0300

Here are some observations about recovery ministries and the church from persons who have done considerable work in this area:

- John Baker says that we need more than para-church organizations doing recovery work; recovery belongs in the church as a mainline ministry. These recovery programs not only help those within the church but also reach out into the community in helping all people deal with their hurts, hang-ups, and habits.

- Dan Stewart, outreach pastor at Calvary Chapel in Newport Mesa, California, talks about the struggles in working with recovery people. He says we need to help them work through their resistance to authority and overcome the victim role. He reminds us that they are sometimes defensive people who don't know how to mourn their losses.

- Tom Sharp, a counselor at Calvary Chapel in Capo Beach, California, urges those working with recovery to cross-reference recovery principles with the Bible. He recommends an integrative approach using church-based recovery ministries. He concludes that we need to build bridges between broken people and the church.

- Gilbert Romero reminds us that bridge building is a multicultural issue. He says that it takes many hands and a great deal of effort to build this bridge. But he warns that it only takes one or two to burn the bridge.

The Need for Continuing Growth

When Sam's sister and her family moved into their present home, there was a beautiful linden tree at the corner of the house. His sister, a horticulturalist, truly appreciated the tree.

But after several years, the leaves were not as full. Even with her knowledge of horticulture, she was unable to diagnose and heal the tree. She sadly watched all the leaves disappear until the tree blew over and died. When she and her husband dug the dead tree out of the ground, they discovered the cause of its demise. The tree had suffered from "root girdling."

As a young tree, it was kept in a large pot. When it grew, the roots reached a limit where they had no room to stretch out, so they grew in circles. At some point the tree was transplanted into the ground. Whoever planted the tree failed to notice the roots growing in circles and didn't spread them out.

As the tree developed, its roots continued to grow in circles. Instead of reaching outward for nutrients in the soil, they grew inwardly. Slowly and surely, the tree strangled itself with its circling roots. The tree died because it was not given room to grow. It had no firm foundation.

This is certainly an accurate parable on spiritual growth. Like the linden tree, we can find ourselves planted within a confining spiritual space, possibly never fully realizing our true potential for growth. We spend our time restrained, only clinging to the same circles instead of extending outward for new spiritual nutrition. Our faith can eventually become stagnant and empty. We too can suffer spiritual decline. Ongoing spiritual growth needs to be a mainstay of every believer. Paul writes:

> *Not that I have already obtained this or have already*
> *reached the goal; but I press on to make it my own,*
> *because Christ Jesus has made me his own. Beloved,*
> *I do not consider that I have made it my own; but this*
> *one thing I do: forgetting what lies behind and straining*
> *forward to what lies ahead, I press on toward the goal*
> *for the prize of the heavenly call of God in Christ Jesus.*
> (Philippians 3:12-14)

The spiritual life is not a destination, but a journey, and it's important not only for people in recovery but for all persons to recognize that reality. Sometimes members of 12-step programs get stuck in the "1-2-3 Shuffle." Christians who are not at all familiar with the 12-steps can experience a similar problem. Instead of growing in spirituality, people merely work and rework the initial steps.

Step One: *We admitted we were powerless over* (fill in the blank with an addiction, problem, etc.), *and that our lives have become unmanageable.* All of us as Christians have an equivalent time when we come to realize that we sin, failing to live as God intended, and do not have the ability to overcome our sin. While this is a crucial step in realizing our need for God's help, continued focus on our sins and failures can make us feel like victimized people with low self-worth.

Step Two: *(We) came to believe that a power greater than us can restore us to sanity.* For all Christians, this means developing faith in Jesus Christ and recognizing his power to change our lives. That experience for many produces a kind of mountain-top emotional experience, in which one is overwhelmed with God's goodness and love. Some Christians fall into the trap of believing that the mountain-top experience should be repeated in every worship service or summer camp or recovery group experience that they have. That's not possible. We continue growing closer to Christ and will have wonderful things happen along the way, but there may be long periods without any strong emotional experiences.

Step Three: *(We) made a decision to turn our will and our lives over to the care of God*. All Christians make a decision to trust their lives to Christ; but once the decision is made, we do not need to continually remake it. Instead we need to focus on following through with what that decision means for our lives.

Really growing in recovery and in the spiritual life means getting beyond the initial steps. Instead of reworking the first three steps repeatedly, people in recovery focus on Steps 10, 11, and 12 as ongoing maintenance steps for spiritual growth. While these steps have been described earlier in detail, let us look at how they work together. Step 10 is about continuous self-examination and confession and often called *Cleaning House.* Step 11 talks about growing intimacy with God by asking only for knowledge of God's will and the power to carry it out. This is often simplified to *Trusting God.* Step 12 urges us to use our spiritual transformation to help others and live a better life. This is simplified to *Helping Others.*

Ongoing growth can be described by these three elements: continuing to clean house, growing trust in God, and finding new ways to help others. These principles are valid for 12-step groups and for the church. As churches take growth in the spiritual life seriously, they seek to provide opportunities to help all people:

- Find support through others in a wide variety of small group experiences which can include Sunday school classes, Bible studies, recovery groups, prayer groups, and fellowship groups.

- Grow in their knowledge of God through study of the Bible, through prayer, and through study of what others have written about the spiritual life. This has implications for what happens in small groups, in worship, and in other settings.

- Identify meaningful opportunities for service both through the church and in the community. While no single church can solve all the social problems found in its geographical area, it's possible for all churches to be involved in some kind of service outreach and to encourage their members to be involved.

- Discover their spiritual gifts and ways to better utilize those in the service of Christ. There are a variety of spiritual gift systems (including one in *Preaching, Planning, and Plumbing* by Steve Clapp, Ron Finney, and Angela Zimmerman) which can assist people in identifying the gifts Christ has given them for service to others.

Both the church and recovery spirituality have the same goal: transforming lives. Their methodology may not always be the same, but it is always accomplished by a program of spiritual growth. In this sense, the gap we are building a bridge over is not that large. We need both churches and 12-step programs as separate entities. But our common goal leads us to work together, compliment each other, and learn from each other whenever possible.

Our approach to the spiritual life is too often one of seeking God's help in doing what we want to do rather than seeking God's will for our lives. Our churches can easily fall into a related trap with those who participate in congregational life. It's easy to focus on recruiting those persons to help meet the institutional needs of the church rather than helping them identify the ministries to which God is calling them–in the church and in the world. Obviously the institutional church needs to be healthy in order to carry out its mission, but nurturing the spiritual lives of those who are part of the body of Christ is fundamental to that mission. When we help people grow spiritually and recognize the service into which Christ is calling them, we discover more energy for healthy congregational life and service to the world than if we stay focused only on institutional health.

---

*God, grant me the serenity
to accept the things I cannot change,
the courage to change the things I can,
and the wisdom to know the difference.
Living one day at a time,
enjoying one moment at a time;
accepting hardship as a pathway to peace;
taking, as Jesus did,
this sinful world as it is,
not as I would have it;
trusting that you will make all things right
if I surrender to your will;
so that I may be reasonably happy in this life
and supremely happy with you forever in the next.
Amen.*

Study Guide

By Angela Zizak

Suggestions for Using this Study Guide

1.   This *Study Guide* is designed for use by individuals and groups wanting to think more deeply about the issues raised in The Church of Recovery. While a few community-based groups may decide to share in this study, most groups will likely be church-based: Sunday school classes, Bible study groups, church boards, membership committees, and mission groups. Some of the activities are clearly more appropriate for use by groups than by individuals.

2.   This *Guide* is designed for twelve sessions–one for each chapter. You may decide to spend more than one session on a chapter, or you may decide to skip some chapters to fit the available time for the topic.

3.   Having class members use different translations of the Bible will enrich your discussion and give new perspective.

4.   The session plans assume that a chalkboard or newsprint is available.

5.   While your sessions will flow better if group members read the chapters in advance, it's not generally wise to assume that all have done so! Give appropriate summaries to help those who have not read the material and to refresh those who have done so.

6.   We recommend that you open and close each session with prayer.

7.   Remember that every group has both active and passive learners.   Try to involve participants in a variety of ways, remaining sensitive to personalities and preferences. Encourage, but do not force, participation. Allow "I pass" as an acceptable response. In this study, some issues may be deeply personal, so we stress the importance of confidentiality within the group.

Session One
Offering Stones to Hungry People, pages 7–20

1. Take some time to discuss the three different church experiences that Ashley went through in her life. How did each one affect Ashley's spiritual and emotional well-being? What do churches do (often unintentionally) to harm the spiritual life? What do they do to develop the spiritual life?

2. On a chalkboard or paper, draw a vertical line down the center. On the left side, list as many factors as the group can that contribute to an unhealthy church (i.e. isolation of people in need, guilt, etc.). On the right, write the factors that contribute to a healthy church (i.e. actively giving love to strangers/newcomers, etc.).

3. Have you ever given someone "stones" when that person was hungry for "food"? In other words, did you give something you thought was needed but that turned out not to be helpful? Why do we often give gifts or advice to people that they really don't need or want? Does it satisfy our need to give more than their needs? How do we know what the appropriate gift is for people?

4. Read Matthew 7: 9-12. Have you always asked for what you needed or wanted? Have you ever been surprised when you got exactly what you asked for, especially when you asked God for something? Have you ever gotten something you thought you didn't want but turned out to be exactly what you needed? Discuss the differences between our "needs" and "wants."

5. How would your church welcome the following people on Sunday morning? Rate the welcome you would expect with "1" being a poor welcome and with "5" being a very warm welcome:

_____ A person with a terminal illness, such as cancer
_____ A single-mother with two small children
_____ A person of different racial or ethnic background
_____ A group of college kids from a nearby university
_____ Two women who arrive holding hands
_____ A person who is dying of AIDS
_____ A person who smells of alcohol and is unclean

Discuss the responses with each other.

141

6. Reflect upon your own church experiences, especially if you have attended more than one church in your lifetime. What sticks out in your mind about the different churches? The people? Their warmth and hospitality? The programs?

Session Two
The Need for Healing, **pages 21–30**

1. How has your faith allowed you to heal when you were sick? when you were stressed? when you felt emotionally depressed or down? Have you ever witnessed someone become physically, mentally, emotionally, or spiritually healed by faith alone? Has this kind of experience changed your perception of faith and healing?

2. Have you ever invited someone to worship? Have you ever been surprised at the impact a simple invitation to worship has on someone? Have you ever witnessed the miracle of Jesus working in the lives of people who desperately needed His help? How has that impacted your own spiritual life–to see the hand of God working on those who seem most downtrodden and fallen? How has this impacted the whole life of the church?

3. John Baker believes that everyone in the church is broken in one way or another. Reflect on the times that you felt broken, depressed, or just let down by someone or by circumstances in life. What did you do to recover (exercise, deeper prayer, medication, talking with a friend, etc.)?

4. Write down a list of all the consequences that can happen as a result of alcoholism (i.e. harm to self on the job; drunk driving kills innocent people, etc.). Now come up with a list of consequences that may accompany other extreme patterns of behavior, such as workaholism, excessive dieting, overuse of prescription drugs, etc. Do any of the consequences match up? Discuss the similarities and differences.

5. Read Matthew 9:35-38. In this passage, Jesus talks about healing as well as sending workers into the harvest fields. How do you connect healing with the harvest? Why are they used in the same context? How can the "harvesters" aid in healing those who need it?

Session Three
The Need for Grace, pages 31–42

1. Some of us in the church are guilty of "works righteousness," where we become highly involved in religious activities in order to "get right with God." Have you ever become too caught up in church activities, leadership roles, or community activities? Have you ever lost sight of why you were committed to these roles in the first place? Has God ever been an after-thought in doing good for others?

2. Reflect upon the statistics given on pages 34–35 about anxiety over money and possessions. Can you include yourself in any of these statistics? Do you work harder or more hours for the opportunity to earn more money? Do you find it hard to give money away, even tithe? Do you still feel impoverished despite having all the material possessions you need? Do you ever alienate yourself from others because you are so intent on satisfying material desires?

3. Do you often compare yourself to others? Do you feel better or worse about yourself? Try asking yourself whether you feel any guilt, shame or self-doubt about yourself. Do you feel haunted by these feelings?

Are you ashamed of something about yourself, your family, or where you came from? Do you feel the need to cover up your shame from others so they don't see or notice it? Share these concerns with the group, if you feel comfortable doing so.

4. Read Ephesians 2:1-10. Discuss the implications of grace through faith and not by works alone. Why is it still important to do good works in the name of Jesus?

5. How has Jesus brought salvation and grace into your life at different times? How did you feel before and after you felt God's presence in your life?

Have you ever provided witness or testimony to others concerning the grace you received from God? Have you ever felt a sense of uplifting by first opening up to others about your sense of brokenness and healing?

6. The "Moral Inventory" on pages 38–39 is really an individual rather than a group activity. If you are doing this study with a group, you might talk together about the issues involved in taking such a thorough moral inventory. Under what circumstances, if any, would you share the results of your inventory with another person? What would you gain from that sharing?

The Church of Recovery

Session Four
The Need for Safe Fellowship, **pages 43–54**

1. Have you ever felt relieved to tell someone a secret about yourself or a problem that you faced? How did you know it was the right time, person, and setting to talk about it? Why was it safe to speak to that person? What factors ensure safety and trust between two or more people? Discuss these factors in the group.

2. What does safety mean to you? What does it mean to different ages of people, such as children, teens and older adults? Make a list separating four different age levels into columns:

    (1) children
    (2) teens
    (3) young to middle-age adults
    (4) older adults
    (5) persons who are shut-ins or in nursing homes

Under each column, create a list of about 10 strategies of how to keep each one safe. (For example, a child is kept safe by being strapped into a car seat; a shut-in may need a home-aid to help with baths.)

Next, make another list of the following groups, again in four columns on another paper:

    (1) a young child who lives in the ghetto
    (2) a teen prostitute
    (3) a young adult drug addict
    (4) an old homeless man on the streets.

List 10 strategies that would ensure safety for each of those people.

Discuss the differences among the lists. Was it harder to come up with some lists than with others? Often we attribute our own experiences to other people, and we may find it difficult to empathize and identify with those who seem radically different.

3. Do you consider your church safe? In what ways? Would your church provide safety to the following people or groups:

Members of a gang who seek to get out of it?
Drug users who are trying to quit?
People who have been in prison?
People of a different sexual orientation?
Runaways or homeless teens?
Isolated elderly (often abandoned by their own families)?
Mentally challenged people?

Think of other groups and discuss how your church could give safety to them.

4. Read Matthew 7:1-2. Why is this message important relative to safety? Why must we be careful about being non-judgmental in order to ensure safety to others?

5. Have you ever heard someone gossip about you? Have you ever participated in gossip? Has your church ever participated in gossip? How does this affect the health and vitality of the church? How does one stop gossip in its tracks? What can we do to heal harmful rifts within the church? Think of specific ways of healing divisions in the church and discuss them in the group.

Session Five
The Need for Integrity, pages 55–62

1. Look the statistics presented on pages 56–57 concerning cheating and dishonesty. Is it surprising that cheating has become so common in society? Does the group agree with the percentages on types of people who cheat? What does that say about our level of trust in these people? Why do we often use the cheating factor as an excuse to not get involved in fighting to "change the system"? Have you or anyone you know ever fought against a formidable challenge and succeeded? Share with the group these experiences.

2. In what ways do we "cheat at church?" List them out on paper or chalkboard. (For example, it could be giving less to the church than a tithe, not being truly welcoming to newcomers, etc.) Do you fall into any of these listed categories? How can you address these things you "cheat on" in church? How can the church as a whole address this issue?

3. Read Psalm 139: 1-4. God knows our thoughts and feelings and whether we are being truthful with ourselves and others. How can we have integrity with others when we are not truthful with ourselves and with God? How can we start to be more truthful with ourselves? Where does this strength come from, especially admitting to ourselves when we have a problem?

4. How does the church deal with confrontation? Is it more painful to deal with open confrontation versus closed or private? Do you describe your church as open to dealing with issues right away, or is your church more passive-aggressive with conflict? How does the church hold itself accountable? Are members honest with one another? Is it easier dealing with some issues and not others? What about dealing with newcomers and some controversial thoughts they may have on church (especially if they have had negative past church experiences)?

Session Six
The Need for Freedom, **pages 63–72**

1. Reflect upon Sam's experience with hiding the hatchet. Have you had a similar experience, in which you were ashamed or embarrassed about telling the truth? Think of other moments in which you were not completely honest with people you loved. What happened to the relationship? Was it ever resolved? If yes, did you feel a sense of freedom or release?

2. Have you ever overdone something (i.e. worked too much, watched too much TV, slept too much, worried too much, etc.)? How did overdoing something impact the other areas of your life? How did it impact other people, especially your loved ones? How did it impact your relationship with God? Did you feel trapped by the excesses?

3. We can get so wrapped up in our lives that we focus too much on earning more money, losing more weight, etc. that our activities enslave us to an empty life. These activities that we do in excess are often thought of as "false idols." What false idols are or were part of your life? Think of times that felt empty to you, and identify what may have contributed to this feeling of emptiness. How can we lose sight of God and his plan for us?

4. Read John 8:31-38. Jesus said that if we hold to his teachings and enact them in our lives, we will be set free. What does it means to be free spiritually?

5. Reflect upon the "Idolatrous Thoughts" on pages 68–70. Are you susceptible to these thoughts from time to time? Have they ever seriously taken over your life? How have they affected your relationship with yourself? With others? With God? How can you keep these thoughts from having too much control over your life?

Session Seven
The Need to Heal Broken Relationships, pages 73–82

1. Has your faith ever wavered when times were tough? Have you always relied upon God for healing broken relationships? Has an estrangement from someone ever caused you to doubt God, or has it brought you closer to God?

2. Resentment is often the root of our anger, guilt, and shame toward others. Make a list of things or people you currently resent in one column. Then in second column, write down WHY you feel resentment. In the third column, write down suggestions for dealing with the resentment (prayer, confronting the person directly, seeking counseling, etc.).

Do you frequently hold a grudge when people hurt you? What about when you hurt others? Do you often seek forgiveness from others?

3. Write a letter to someone with whom you have an unresolved issue or toward whom you feel resentment. This might be a child, spouse, sibling, parent, friend, co-worker, or neighbor. Feel free to pour out your feelings and thoughts on paper, regardless of how you think the other person would react. Be sure to use "I" statements, such as "I think" and "I feel," owning up to your own feelings and not blaming someone else for the way you feel.

Remember: it's natural to feel guilt, shame, anger, and resentment. Just get it out! This is simply an exercise to release resentment or any negative feelings.

Think carefully before actually sending such a letter. A personal conversation may be a better way to heal the relationship. It may also not be the right time to attempt healing.

4. Read Psalm 34: 17-18; Psalm 51:17. Is it comforting knowing that God will always be there for us, especially in our saddest, darkest moments? Discuss with the group, if you wish, a sad or dark moment in your life. Perhaps a close loved one passed away, or something happened to make you feel like an absolute failure. Explore what you felt then and how you got through these tough times. Who helped you and how? Have you ever helped someone get out of their own dark moment?

5. Pray a "Resentment Prayer" (described on pages 80–81). This is not a group activity, though you may want to talk about the experience.

Session Eight
Intimacy with God, **pages 83-90**

1. Think of the moments in your life that you felt most at peace with yourself, the people you were with, and your life in general. Then think of the times you felt closest in your relationship with God. Do you feel those moments often coincide? Does being at peace with yourself always mean intimacy with God? Why, or why not?

2. How can we call upon God to transform our lives into greater mission and service? Why do we resist God's transforming power at times? Why are we afraid of intimacy with God? Where does this fear stem from? How can we overcome this fear and develop a deeper relationship with God?

3. People with substance addictions often start or continue their destructive patterns because they want to fill in the void in their lives. How can we recognize that there is a void in our lives in the first place? How can we recognize the signs that we are using the wrong "substances" to fill our void? How can we recognize the void in others and what they do to fill that void in their lives?

4. Read John 15:12-17. Imagine the reactions from Jesus' followers when he said they were his friends and not merely his servants. Do you have a close personal friendship with Jesus? Do you see him as a friend, a sibling, a parent, a mentor, a teacher, a judge, or a master? What words would you use to describe your relationship with Christ?

5. Prayer, meditation, study, mentoring, and a support group are good ways to become more intimate with God. Share with the group other ways to be intimate, including methods that you personally use. For example:

> Exercise
> Yoga
> Being outside in a beautiful natural setting
> Being totally alone
> Planting a garden
> Making music

Sometimes obtaining faith is easier that maintaining it. How do we develop a deeper spiritual life?

6. To close, have the group share the "Serenity Prayer" on pages 87–88.

Session Nine
The Need for Spiritual Power, **pages 91–102**

1. Reflect upon the four messages that Elizabeth received about life, as listed on page 92. Have you ever been a victim of these kinds of thoughts? How did it feel to give up these thoughts and rely on God? Can you empathize with the people described on page 94–95?

2. What painful experiences (death of a loved one, divorce, lost job, etc.) have profoundly affected your own spiritual power? How did you overcome your ordeal and work through your emotions? Did you get help from others, from God through prayer?

3. Read 2 Corinthians 12:9-10. Discuss the paradoxes in this message–in which weakness is power in the eyes of the Lord. How does this have relevance to our society today, when we our society rewards strength, power, competition, and prestige? Explore how we can be humble and respectful despite the sometimes overwhelming desire to be "on top."

4. Accountability is an interesting concept. Businesses hold themselves accountable through quality control and work reviews. Friends and family discuss issues with loved ones so they don't harm themselves or others. How do you hold yourself accountable?

Session Ten
The Need to Serve Others, **pages 103–112**

1. How do we serve others if we don't fully comprehend the needs they have or problems they are facing? How do you address people you do not know very well with the problems that are evident? Particularly, how do you reach strangers who need Christ, especially in their own healing? Why is it often necessary to develop a relationship before attempting to help someone?

2. What does "service" mean? Define the different uses and arenas of service. Have you ever been served by someone (not just in a restaurant)? Have you ever served others yourself? How does it feel to know exactly what someone is going through because you had the same experience? How does it feel when you never had it?

3. Has serving others ever given you new life, ever lifted you out of depression or self-absorption? Share with the group your past and present service experiences (i.e. hosting an exchange student, fostering a child, mentoring or tutoring, building homes for Habitat for Humanity, soup kitchen, etc.).

How does the church become highly involved in community service? What dangers come when the church is self-centered or self-absorbed?

4. Read Mark 10:42-45; John 13: 1-17. Jesus is described as the ultimate servant and clearly showed his love for his friends and disciples. He also gave an example of what we are all to do. How do we practice this kind of servanthood? Do we have to work in a soup kitchen in order to be a servant?

5. Discuss arenas and people whom we can serve, besides family, friends, and the church. Discuss ways with the group that your church can expand its ministries.

Session Eleven
The Need to Carry the Message, **pages 113_124**

1. Why "carry" the message? What is so significant about carrying something? What does it mean? A definition could be that to carry something means to transfer something from one place to another. What we learn from one place we bring somewhere else, continually transferring what we hear and learn to others. Discuss ways that members of the group have "carried" the message of Jesus.

2. Have you ever played the telephone game? Everyone sits in a circle and one person starts by saying a phrase, whispering it to the next person. After going around the entire circle, the initial message often becomes very different, depending on how many people are involved and how they interpreted it.

How does the message of Jesus become distorted like this? What distractions (internal or external) and interpretations cause it to become different? How do you keep it from becoming distorted as we carry it to others?

3. Evangelism is the primary way of attracting people to Jesus. What approach do you use personally? What does the church primarily use? Come up with new ways you and the church can use to bring the message to people and then implement them during the next several months. See what happens to the life of your church! (See Steve Clapp and Fred Bernhard's book *Widening the Welcome of Your Church* for some suggestions.)

4. Examine the research statistics on church growth on pages 117–118. What kind of training does your church offer people to help them share their faith?

Sometimes we unintentionally say things to others we don't mean. What we say, and especially HOW we say it, can have a big impact on how others interpret the message. Identify ways you and the church may say things that might turn someone off to the message of Jesus. What improvements can be made?

5. Faith is the heart of this chapter. How do you communicate your faith to someone who is an atheist? Or an agnostic? Or a non-religious Christian? Or a Christian from a different denomination or faith tradition? Is the approach different for

each person? Reflect on the strategies of sharing the faith on pages 120–124.

6. Read Matthew 17:20-21; Romans 10:6-13. These passages describe faith in doing the impossible, including carrying the message of Jesus. What confidence is shown in spreading the word of God! After reading these passages, pray for the guidance and confidence to give witness to God's word to others.

Session Twelve
Building Bridges, **pages 125–137**

1. How do we become restrained from building bridges to others? What causes our fears about reaching out to others and spanning the gap? How can a new bridge be built to reach others when the church itself is in decline? Is it easier for a growing church to build bridges? Why, or why not? How have you built bridges between yourself and others? Between the church and the community?

2. What does "user-friendly" mean? Often that term is associated with computers. Discuss ways your church can be more user-friendly to kids under 12-years-old, to teens, to young adults between the ages of 20-30, to adults, to elderly adults (over 65), to the homebound and sick. How can the church help meet the needs of each of these age groups?

3. What gifts do people in your church have for starting a recovery group or program in the church? How can the people and facilities be used to bring healing–especially spiritual healing–to others? Openly explore different avenues to bring healing to others through your church. Which ideas should be put into action? What are the next steps?

4. Read 1 Corinthians 3:7-17. We are temples in which God dwells. He gives us strength, faith, and hope that we can be bridges to lead other people to him. After reading the passage, pray for God's grace in helping you connect with others to pass on God's message of hope and love.

Resources

Resources referred to in this book:

Baker, John, *Celebrate Recovery.* Zondervan, 1998.

Bernhard, Fred and Steve Clapp, *Widening the Welcome of Your Church.* LifeQuest, 1996, 1997, 1999.

Bontrager, Ed, *Following in the Footsteps of Paul.* Mennonite Publishing House, 1994.

Clapp, Steve and Sam Detwiler, *Sharing Living Water.* LifeQuest, 1996, 2000, 2001.

The Dalai Lama, *The Art of Happiness.* Riverhead Books, 1998.

Hershey, S. Joan, *Forever in Love.* Engle Publishing, 2000.

Hershey, Terry, *Go Away, Come Closer.* Word Publishing, 1990.

Lamott, Anne, *Crooked Little Heart.* Anchor/Random House, 1997.

Lamott, Anne, *Traveling Mercies.* Anchor/Random House, 1999.

Lewis, C.S., *Mere Christianity.* Macmillan, 1943, 1945, 1952.

Miller, J. Keith, *The Secret Life of the Soul,* Broadman & Holman Publishers, 1997.

Moore, Thomas, *Meditations.* HarperSanFrancisco, 1995.

Newby, R., *Sacred Chaos and the Quest for Spiritual Intimacy,* Continuum Publishing Co., 1998.

Nouwen, Henri J.M., *In the Name of Jesus.* Crossroad, 1994.

Scott, Dan, *The Emerging American Church.* Bristol Books, 1993,

Alcoholics Anonymous. World Services, Inc., 1976.

Other resources available from LifeQuest on church outreach and hospitality:

*Bernhard, Fred and Steve Clapp, *Widening the Welcome of Your Church*, 1996, 1997, 1999, 2000. A very practical book which shows how biblical hospitality can revitalize a congregation. For individual reading or group study.

*Clapp, Steve, *Overcoming Barriers to Church Growth*, 1994. For people who have difficulty getting the congregation interested in outreach. Includes a very helpful section on low self-esteem in individuals, congregations, and denominations as a sometimes overlooked barrier.

Clapp, Steve and Fred Bernhard. *Hospitality: Life in a Time of Fear.* Deals with the fears that pervade our society in the wake of September 11, 2001, and shows how biblical hospitality can help us move past our fears. Hospitality is presented not as a church program but as a way of life which grows out of our spirituality.

*Detwiler, Sam and Steve Clapp, *Sharing Living Water*, 1996, 2000, 2001. How to share the faith in comfortable, nonmanipulative ways. For individual reading or group study.

*Hershey, S. Joan, *The First Thirty Seconds: A Guide to Hospitality for Greeters and Ushers*, 2000. Gives practical strategies to help church greeters and ushers, who are on the front lines of hospitality, create a warm experience for all who come.

Hershey, S. Joan and Steve Clapp, *Healthy Pastor–Healthy Church.* Practical suggestions for improving the health and the effectiveness of pastors.

For information about quantity orders of this publication or about our other resources, contact:

LifeQuest and Christian Community
6404 S. Calhoun Street • Fort Wayne, IN 46807 • U.S.A.
219-744-6510 (General Inquiries) • 419-872-7448 (Orders)
DadofTia@aol.com • www.churchstuff.